Peace

in the
Midst

A Devotional Passport
to Peace

To Kathy,

Joyfully,

Carol

CAROL HOPSON

WINEPRESS WP PUBLISHING

ISBN 1-57921-342-1
Library of Congress Catalog Card Number: 00-110383

What God Is Doing
Through Carol Hopson's Books

The unfolding of Thy words gives light; it gives understanding to the simple. —Psalm 119:130 NASB

From Sue:

Please keep writing! Your books have reached my heart like no others, and I read a lot. I think it's because they're so practical, and they have so much Scripture in them. I also appreciate how honest you are about your struggles. I've finally stopped feeling like a victim and am learning to live in victory. I've also learned that my choices each day make all the difference. Thanks for your obedience to the Lord.

From Alice:

I've never read a book that touched my heart so specifically as yours. It was like you were living in my skin, and I couldn't believe what I was reading because it was my story. The problem is, I didn't choose to accept it and grow with it but became discouraged and disillusioned about my faith. Thank you for showing me the way back and where I got off track. I can't wait to share your book with my family and friends.

From Natalie:

*I saw your book, **But God, I'm Tired of Waiting!** in the bookstore and just had to get it. I am so tired of waiting for things and people to change. I keep expecting God to do something that makes sense to me, and I've been getting so discouraged because things just aren't happening like I want them to. As I read your book, the tears began to flow. I realized that I was telling God what to do rather than being His servant and allowing Him to use me in my situation. It has totally changed my outlook, and now I focus on pleasing Him and growing each day. I'm leaving the rest with Him.*

From Ed:
My wife brought your book home after hearing you at a women's retreat. I usually don't read her books, but she said this one might help me as I was really depressed with losing my job. I couldn't get a grip on what God was doing. After reading **But God, This Wasn't My Plan!** I recognized my problem and was able to get back on track with the Lord. Thanks for your honesty and faithfulness to write this book. I'm one man who is grateful my wife went to your retreat.

From Debbie:
I read **But God, I'm Tired of Waiting!** three times. I couldn't believe you had the exact same feelings I had, but I didn't know where to go or what to do. Your book was so practical and helpful and one of the most inspirational books I've ever read. I have purchased ten more to share with my friends who are struggling. Thank you for your transparency and your obedience. It's truly inspiring.

From Sheila:
I didn't realize how bitter I had become until I read the chapter "I Must Let Go of the Hurt!" in **But God, I'm Tired of Waiting!** The Lord totally convicted me, and I had to confess layers and layers of anger and bitterness. I can't thank you and the Lord enough for helping me be free to love, forgive, and live for God again.

From Karen:
I was handed your book, **But God, This Wasn't My Plan!** at a very crucial time in my life. My husband had been unjustly relieved from his pastoral position, and we were devastated. A friend bought the book for herself, but after seeing my pain, she gave it to me. It saved my life! Your "Facing Fear with Faith" chapter was exactly what I needed. I read it over and over and claimed the Scriptures for my own. I can't believe God knew the depths of my despair and had you write this book.
Oh give thanks to the Lord . . . Make known His deeds among the peoples. —Psalm 105:1 NASB

This book is dedicated
to
my children

Jeff and Adriana Hopson
and
Joel and Jennifer Miller

with great love for
who you are
and
deepest thanks
for giving me

Monica, Rebecca,
Elliot, Jack, and
Lucy Marie.

I love you!

Contents

INTRODUCTION: ix

CHAPTER 1: Choosing to Love God's Word 13

CHAPTER 2: Choosing Daily Fellowship and Obedience . . 21

    Day 1: What Are You Choosing? 23

    Day 2: Where Are Your Eyes? 27

    Day 3: Are You Changing Seasons? 30

    Day 4: What About Your Heart? 35

    Day 5: Is Your Shield in Place? 38

    Day 6: You're One Day Closer! 41

    Day 7: The Good Thing Is! 44

    Day 8: Can You Know God's Will? 47

    Day 9: Are You Waiting Patiently? 50

    Day 10: Are You Singing Today? 53

Day 11: How About Some Weed Pulling? 56

Day 12: Are You Capturing Your Thoughts? 59

Day 13: Are You Thankful for Small Things? 63

Day 14: It's Never Easy! 66

Day 15: What Kind of Trophy Are You? 70

Day 16: Is Your Daddy There? 73

Day 17: God Is in Control! 76

Day 18: Are You Tired Today? 79

Day 19: Have You Found Contentment? 82

Day 20: What Matters to God? 86

Day 21: What Voice Do You Listen to? 90

Day 22: How About a New Point of View? 93

Day 23: Trust When You Can't Understand! 96

Day 24: Are You Yelling or Listening? 99

Day 25: Did You Let the Thief in? 102

Day 26: Are You Bringing Joy to Your Father? 106

Day 27: Does My Attitude Matter? 109

Day 28: Do You Have an Idol? 112

Day 29: You're Very Special! 115

Day 30: Are You Fretting? 119

CHAPTER 3: Choosing a New Way of Life! 123

EPILOGUE 135

INDEX OF POEMS 138

INTRODUCTION

"I'm so miserable!" she cried. "My husband's job brought us here, but I hate it! All my friends are back East, and I'm so lonely. All I can think of is moving back. The kids are upset, I'm a mess, I'm furious with my husband for moving us here, and I feel so hopeless."

Sitting there with Gina, I thought of the many times that I'd heard this same type of heart cry from other women. Things were going along just fine until a sudden circumstance brought unwanted changes, and they weren't ready for them. Is there hope for Gina? Is peace really a choice for her?

Ellen just found out her beloved, Christian daughter is pregnant and unmarried. Ellen didn't even know the girl had a boyfriend. She feels her heart has been ripped out, and life will never be happy again. As I listened, my heart went out to her, and I was overwhelmed by her grief and despair. Was this really the end of peace for Ellen and her daughter?

It's been quite a week for my husband and me. We just found out that my dad's cancer has returned, and my mother has a life-threatening blood clot, which wasn't found on her many visits to the doctor in the last six months. Another call came informing us that my father-in-law was having emergency surgery on his carotid artery that was ninety-nine percent blocked. As I flew north to be with my parents and my husband flew to Idaho to be with his father, I asked God to give me that peace that He promises in His precious Word, *the peace . . . which surpasses all comprehension* (Philippians 4:7).

Is peace only a possibility, a passing thought, or a promise from our heavenly Father? Could I tell Gina and Ellen that peace was definitely available to them? They were Christians but were not experiencing peace in their circumstances. Could I claim that promised peace with both my parents and my father-in-law facing critical health problems?

As I reflected on the Scriptures I had committed to memory many years ago, I was reminded that:

Those who love Thy law have great peace, and nothing causes them to stumble.
—Psalm 119:165

The steadfast of mind Thou wilt keep in perfect peace, because he trusts in Thee.
—Isaiah 26:3

Be anxious for nothing, but in everything by prayer and supplication with thanksgiving let your requests be made known to God. And the peace of God, which surpasses which all comprehension, shall guard your hearts and minds in Christ Jesus.

—Philippians 4:6–7

In the following pages, we will examine the Scriptures and find the secret to peace in any situation. We will see how Gina and Ellen found peace, and *we will discover whether peace is determined by our circumstances or by our choices.*

Help Me, Lord

Dear God, I want Your peace so much,
my heart is wrenched with pain.
I feel alone and out of touch.
My fears have left me drained.

I want to live a peaceful life,
one that honors You.
But things seem so beyond control,
I don't know what to do.

Is there peace for one like me?
Do You really care?
Please show me now what I should do,
and let me know You're there.

"My child, I've never left your side.
You're loved more than you know.
But I have given you a choice.
Now which way will you go?"

—*Carol Hopson*

CHAPTER 1

CHOOSING TO LOVE GOD'S WORD

*Those who love Thy law
have great peace, and nothing causes them to stumble.*
— Ps. 119:165

Amazing! Is this saying that if we love God's Word, nothing will remove our peace or cause us to stumble? It seems clear to me, and yet so many times we don't have God's peace. Why is that? I think we don't understand what it means to love God and His Word.

When Jeff fell in love with Adriana, nothing else was important anymore. Every thought was of her and when he could be with her again. The phone calls to her were endless, and everything had a new purpose. His job was a means to have money to take Adriana out and buy her gifts. His life had a new purpose—to spend as much time with her as he possibly could and pray that one day she would become his wife. It was a drastic life change for Jeff whose love before that had been sports, all kinds of sports. Suddenly, Jeff worked longer hours, took on extra jobs, whistled while he worked, and kissed his mother more often. How do I know this about Jeff? He's my son.

Everything changed when Adriana entered his life, and he was never the same again. It was a wonderful change, but what brought it about? Love, pure and simple. When Jeff fell in love, the whole world looked different to him. You see, he no longer was interested in any other girls. His goal was to get to know and love this one girl in every way possible. His total desire was to please her, be a better man for her, and spend as much time as he could with her. He would often call me by her name because she was constantly on his mind. I think you're getting the picture.

This, then, is what true love is like. It's total commitment to the one we love, forsaking all others. I'd like to share a perspective on loving the Lord and His Word in this way so we have great peace. Let's look at it in the following way:

L-etting go of everything else

O-beying at any cost

V-aluing God and His Word above all

E-xperiencing the joy

Letting Go of Everything Else

When Jeff fell in love with Adriana, he never desired anyone else. When we give our hearts and lives to the Lord, we should not desire our old loves, but we often lose our peace because of going back to the old ways.

Therefore consider the members of your earthly body as dead to immorality, impurity, passion, evil desire, and greed, which amounts to idolatry . . . But now you also, put them all aside: anger, wrath, malice, slander, and abusive speech from your mouth. (Col. 3:5, 8)

When I have lost my peace, it is because I have gone back to the old way of thinking and have left my first love. Sometimes I am angry because things have not gone as I wanted them to, and I lose my peace. Sometimes I've said something I shouldn't have, and my peace is gone because of a broken relationship. Maybe someone has said critical words to me, and it's difficult to forgive. Other times, my desires have not been in line with what the Lord wants for me, and so I am disgruntled, and self-centered thoughts eat away at my peace. It's no wonder I'm miserable. I am not loving the Word! If I were, I would let go of my ways and go with what the Word says.

And so, as those who have been chosen of God, holy and beloved, put on a heart of compassion, kindness, humility, gentleness and patience; bearing with one another, and forgiving each other, whoever has a complaint against anyone; just as the Lord forgave you, so also should you. And beyond all these things put on love, which is the perfect bond of unity. And let the peace of Christ rule in your hearts, to which indeed you were called in one body; and be thankful. (Col. 3: 12–15)

"Those who love Thy law have great peace" means we accept and love what it teaches more than we love our own ways.

Obeying at Any Cost

Three lonely, single women lived in a western town. One day, a traveling salesman who sold magic mirrors came to town. "Come and buy your magic mirror, and your life will never be the same!" he hollered for all to hear. The three women listened, and each decided to purchase a miracle-working mirror. So they took their mirrors home and waited for miracles.

The first woman put her mirror in a drawer. After a few weeks, she was angry and bitter that nothing wonderful or magical had happened, so she threw her mirror away.

The second woman hung her mirror on the back porch and glanced at it when she walked by but didn't pay much attention to it. She, too, became disgruntled with it since nothing changed in her dull, lonely life.

The third woman decided this must be a very special mirror. She hung it by the front door and admired it each time she went in or out the door. As she gazed intently at the image in the magic mirror one day, she noticed her clothes looked shabby and wrinkled. Maybe she should wash them more often and iron them before she wore them. A few days later, she noticed that her hair seemed unkempt, so she brushed it more and tried a new hairstyle. At the same time, she thought a little makeup could make her cheeks look rosier and healthier. Eventually, she tried smiling into the new purchase and was shocked to see how her face changed when she smiled. So she decided she would try smiling more often.

Soon the third woman had male suitors calling on her, and eventually one asked for her hand in marriage. "My, my!" she exclaimed. "I certainly am glad I bought that magic mirror. It has changed my life!"

Don't only hear the message, but put it into practice; otherwise you are merely deluding yourselves. The man who simply hears and does nothing about it is like a man catching the reflection of his natural face in a mirror. He sees himself, it is true, but he goes off without the slightest recollection of what sort of person he saw in the mirror. But the man who looks into the perfect law, the law of liberty, and makes a habit of so doing, is not the man who hears and forgets. He puts that law into practice and he wins true happiness. (James 1:23–25 Phillips)

When we truly love God's Word, we put God's "law into practice" at any cost and find true peace and happiness.

Valuing God and His Word Above All Else

To reflect once more on Jeff and his love for Adriana, it was obvious that he valued her more than his own life. Whatever made her happy was what he wanted, and his desires took a backseat. If she wanted to take a walk rather than watch an important football game, that's what he did. And he did it with great joy! If she wanted to go shopping, Jeff suddenly found shopping interesting and fun because it made her happy.

When I value the truths of God's Word above all else, I put them into practice in my life and pay no attention to my human, self-centered desires. If I pursue my desire to be angry, frustrated, or worried, then I have made a choice to love myself first.

Let me explain. Recently, my husband kindly asked if I would mind having a business friend stay with us for a few days that month. I knew that this was important to him, or he wouldn't have asked. Usually, I love company, but this particular month was already full with speaking at two retreats, several church luncheons, another trip, writing, and discipling women. My response was not what it should have been as I replied with my weary, selfish emotions rather than with love. I reminded him of my schedule and all I was doing to help others. I just didn't need this extra burden right now.

As I sat there in silence, knowing that I had attacked him rather than lovingly thinking it through, I knew I needed to do what the Lord wanted, but what was it? Would you believe I had just read 1 Peter 4:8 and 9 that very morning? It reads, *Above all, keep fervent in your love for one another, because love covers a multitude of sins. Be hospitable to one another without complaint.* Okay, did I value my rights or God's words more? You might be thinking, "But you had a right to say no because you were busy, and he should have been more thoughtful." It's important for you to know that my husband is thoughtful and protective of me and my schedule, but I had not given him time to explain how this would all work out because I put my feelings first.

To restore peace to my heart and to our relationship, I needed to be fervent in my love for my husband while discussing this, and I needed to be willing to be hospitable to his friend without complaint. It was totally possible as I thought about it and not nearly as difficult as I had made it. God's Word directly convicted me, and my heart was at peace again when I apologized for my attitude and opened my heart to what my husband asked of me. To value God's Word above all else brings peace.

Experiencing the Joy

Oh, the joy of being in love! You know, I never had to tell my son to be happy or to cheer up before he left for a date. The anticipation of being together and the joy of the relationship was all he needed to be happy. Are you experiencing the joy of knowing and loving the Lord and His precious Word? When I really focus on the Word and decide to obey it, I experience the joy that comes from my unbroken relationship with my Lord.

And these things we write, so that our joy may be made complete (1 John 1:4). It's obedience to God's Word that makes our joy complete, but we so often listen to other voices—voices that appeal to our old loves. Again we are reminded: *If you keep My commandments, you will abide in My love; just as I have kept My Father's commandments, and abide in His love. These things I have spoken to you, that My joy may be in you, and that your joy may be made full* (John 1:10–11).

As I look carefully at these passages, I see that our Lord Jesus Christ will put His joy in us as we keep His Word. The purpose of His instructions for our thoughts and behavior is not only to glorify Himself but to bring us joy in our obedience. The problem is that this thought goes against everything that today's media and culture teaches us. That's why we are warned that *"our battle is to bring down every deceptive fantasy and every imposing defense that men erect against the true knowledge of God. We even fight to capture every thought until it acknowledges the authority of Christ"* (2 Cor. 10:5 Phillips).

The Word of God

Your precious Word!
Gives me insight, makes me wise, better than gold.
I lay down my load.

Your precious Word!
Is righteousness, convicts of sin, sheds new light.
Help me not fight.

Your precious Word!
Brings me joy, revives my soul, gives me peace.
My will I release.

Your precious Word!
Reaches my heart, meets my needs, lights my way!
Help me obey.

—*Carol Hopson*

CHAPTER 2

CHOOSING DAILY FELLOWSHIP AND OBEDIENCE

Now it gets personal! Are you ready to take every thought captive to the obedience of Christ? If you have decided that you want to live in obedience to God's Word and discover how to live in peace, then this next section is for you.

Since peace is found through truly loving God and His Word, this section takes you through one or more portions of Scripture each day and helps you apply it in your daily life. There is a poem for insight and questions for reflection and obedience. It is my prayer that as you focus on the truths of God's Word and the power of His presence in your life, you will learn to *choose* the peace God offers you.

The steadfast of mind Thou wilt keep in perfect peace, because he trusts in Thee. (Isa. 26:3)

~Day 1~
WHAT ARE YOU CHOOSING?

No soldier in active service entangles himself in the affairs of everyday life, so that he may please the one who enlisted him as a soldier. (2 Tim. 2:4)

Have you enlisted in God's army? Have you signed up for duty by accepting Jesus as your Lord and Savior? Then you are in active service! The things that will entangle you today will be your own choices, which remove you from *active service.*

Those choices might be to be consumed with worry, to be frustrated with your circumstances, to be unforgiving, to allow bitterness to grow, to neglect your personal time with the Lord, or to dwell on what you don't have. As this verse reminds us, while entangled in these things, we cannot please the Lord. Therefore, we're not fulfilling the purpose for which we were created, and we have no peace.

When God moved me from a warm, sunny climate to a dark, rainy one, I had to make a choice each day if I was to have peace. When He chose to move me away from my children and four precious grandchildren, I had to make a choice. I could trust that God had a purpose for this change because He loves me and wants to use me. Or I could choose to think this was an unbearable situation I couldn't possibly deal with. **My choice, not my circumstances, determined my peace or lack of it.** Can you see how your choices are affecting the peace God freely offers?

Remember this promise, *The Lord will bless His people with peace* (Ps. 29:11). *Choose for yourselves today whom you will serve* (Josh. 24:15). **Are you serving self or the Savior today?**

Choices

I have a choice to make today;
the sky is oh so dark,
and I'm so used to sunny days
and walking in the park.

In sunshine there's so much to do,
but what to do in rain?
I don't think that the Lord's idea
is to sit and just complain!

What blessings can I claim right now
when outside grows so dim?
Is happiness a product of sun
or a relationship with Him?

I know God gives me choices
that will change my attitude.
I know I need to look to Him
to show me what to do.

I think I'll choose obedience
and get my will in line.
There's reading, writing, and calls to make
and making the most of my time.

I called a friend whose faith grew dim
and reminded her to trust
and realized that on gloomy days
helping others is a must.

I wrote some notes of encouragement
to those I felt in need,
and read a chapter in the Book,
my hungry soul to feed.

And then I took a walk to see
a neighbor on my street.
How could I be God's servant if
my neighbors I never meet?

Her lonely heart was yearning
for someone who really cared.
But had it been a sunny day
I might have not been there.

There's something God is teaching me
about these days of rain,
to let Him fill my days with joy
and from discontent refrain.

—*Carol Hopson*

Questions for Reflection and Obedience

1. Have you made a commitment of your life, your dreams, your service to the Lord?

2. What is entangling you and causing you to worry, to fear, or to be frustrated, removing you from active service?

3. Why haven't you given this burden to the Lord and left it there? (Be honest and specific.)

4. Read Philippians 1:6 and 20, then write a commitment to the Lord about how you will try, with His help, to make a godly choice in your situation.

5. Pray through your commitment, confess your weaknesses, and then seek God's help to be faithful to your promise.

~Day 2~
WHERE ARE YOUR EYES?

Therefore, since we have so great a cloud of witnesses surrounding us, let us also lay aside every encumbrance, and the sin which so easily entangles us, and let us run with endurance the race that is set before us, fixing our eyes on Jesus, the author and perfecter of faith, who for the joy set before Him endured the cross, despising the shame, and has sat down at the right hand of the throne of God. (Heb. 12:1–2)

It was so much fun to watch my son and daughter fall in love with their future mates. When they were together after a long absence, their eyes were literally fixed on each other. Their gazes were filled with love, reassurance, treasured smiles, unspoken words, and the unspeakable joy of knowing each others' hearts. How they anticipated the future joy of being united in marriage.

This, then, is the way we should fix our eyes on Jesus. It is only through Him that our deepest needs are met. He alone loves us unconditionally and reassures us of our worth through His Word. He knows our thoughts and motives and is intimately acquainted with all our ways (Ps. 139:1–6). Our future is found in Him, and our purpose is fulfilled *only* by living to glorify Him.

So why do we look elsewhere for peace and fulfillment? Because we've taken our eyes off the One we love, and we think that someone else can meet our emotional needs. You see, we don't receive the positive spiritual feedback we gain by looking to Jesus because we have turned our eyes in another direction. This usually leads to discouragement and unfulfilled expectations.

Jesus will never disappoint you. He needs to be your first love. He alone can bring peace, self-worth, and comfort. **Where are your eyes today?**

Lord of the Dance

At first I didn't know the steps
my Father sought to teach
for training in the dance of life
when He said He would lead.

Sometimes I would follow Him
and take His hand in mine.
Other times I looked aside;
my steps were out of line.

Each lesson grew more intricate
between my Lord and me.
And I began to understand
that His face held the key.

For when I kept my eyes on Him
and looked into His face,
My heart was free of doubt and fear
and wrong steps were erased.

So now I'll let Him take the lead
and look not left or right.
Then peace will come as eye to eye
I dance without a fight.

—*Carol Hopson*

Questions for Reflection and Obedience

1. What circumstances usually take your eyes off of Jesus?

2. What happens when you look anywhere else for reassurance or fulfillment?

3. Are you usually aware that you have changed your focus?

4. What will you change in the following areas to help keep your eyes fixed on Jesus? (Use Philippians 4:6–8; Colossians 3:2; 2 Timothy 1:12.)

    Your time with the Lord:

    Your thought life:

    People you spend time with:

5. What Scriptures will you "set before" you to help you?

~Day 3~
ARE YOU CHANGING SEASONS?

There is an appointed time for everything. And there is a time for every event under heaven. (Eccles. 3:1)

I tend to look at my life like a book with many chapters. The ones that are already written have very full pages; some are filled with great joy and ministry, while others have changed plans, discouragement, and opportunities for growth. Each chapter represents a season in my life, a season that I usually want to hang on to. You know how it is! You get comfortable in your season, and you don't want it to change. But changes come . . .

- You have to move
- You lose your job
- Your heart has been broken
- You're facing new health problems
- Your children leave home

And you don't want to let go and enter a new chapter! Hanging onto a season that God has chosen or allowed to end destroys our peace.

I've got my eye on the goal, where God is beckoning us onward—to Jesus. I'm off and running, and I'm not turning back. So let's keep focused on that goal, those of us who want everything God has for us. If any of you have something else in mind, something less than total commitment, God will clear your blurred vision—you'll see it yet! (Phil. 3:13–15 The Message)

Instead of realizing that the next chapter could have new joys and unexpected surprises in it, we refuse to open our hearts to God's plan. I've found that when I finally let go, turn the page, and look to the future with anticipation and trust, I've always been surprised by God's grace, sufficiency, and wondrous plan.

Do you want everything God has for you? Sometimes it means entering a new season, one that is uncomfortable and unknown but filled with new opportunities for growth and service.

Seasons

I woke one day and found that I
was in a brand new season.
It took me by surprise and so
I didn't like the reason.

It wasn't what was comfortable
and not what I would choose.
I didn't want my life to change,
I had so much to lose.

This season brought uncertainty
on almost every side.
I couldn't cling to things on earth
or in my friends confide.

Humility and patience were
the clothes I needed now
to get me through this trying time,
but God would teach me how.

To wear them daily for my Lord
and thank Him for His Word
and trust that God's sufficiency
from my mouth would be heard.

For as I chose humility,
pride had to step aside.
And Satan had no power then
so had to run and hide.

And how could he cause me to fret
if patience was my choice?
He couldn't have a victory
'cause praise rang through my voice.

And then the overcoat of peace
protected from the cold
And kept my heart both soft and warm
and easier to mold.

So in this season of my life
I trust my Father still,
For nothing comes to me without
first passing through His will.

—*Carol Hopson*

Questions for Reflection and Obedience

1. Describe the season you are having difficulty leaving behind:

2. Why is the season you are entering difficult for you?

3. What hinders you from believing that God can take care of you and give you joy in this new season?

4. Do you realize that your answer to number 3 is the sin of unbelief?

5. How can you use Philippians 4:19 and 2 Corinthians 9:8 to help you change your attitude?

~Day 4~
WHAT ABOUT YOUR HEART?

Do nothing from selfishness or empty conceit, but with humility of mind let each of you regard one another as more important than himself; do not merely look out for your own personal interests, but also for the interests of others. (Phil. 2:3–4)

Is your heart in turmoil today? If so, who are you thinking about? I remember a difficult time in my life when a long-time, trusted friend betrayed me. The pain was almost unbearable. The more I thought about how much it hurt and how unfair the situation was, the worse I felt (Ps. 32:2–5). I couldn't feel God's peace when I was so miserable.

Through reading God's Word, I realized that my focus was on me, not others. I was consumed with my pain and so was not reaching out to help others.

When we become self-centered, we can't see the needs around us, and we allow evil thoughts to overcome us. Romans 12:21 reminds us, *Do not be overcome by evil, but overcome evil with good.*

When I finally opened my heart to what God was trying to show me, He led me to begin a new ministry that would help others. And so I opened my home to women who were in pain by starting a new evening Bible study for widowed, divorced, or abandoned women.

What a blessing those Tuesday evenings turned out to be! God had already prepared many hearts to come, and though I felt inadequate for the task, He was always faithful. By leaving my pain in God's hands and reaching out to help others, my problem faded into the background, and God's joy and peace surfaced once again.

A Servant's Heart

Do I have a servant's heart,
or do I seek attention
for things I do in ministry
that someone might not mention?

Do I seek to help someone
whose heart is filled with pain?
Or am I only moved to act
by something I might gain?

Do I let the Holy Spirit
guide my deeds and thoughts each day?
Or do I contemplate a need
then go my selfish way?

Do I see with Jesus' eyes
those near me in despair?
Do I understand God's purpose
is for me to show His care?

Do I have a servant's heart
as I go about today?
Will I truly please my Savior?
As He leads, will I obey?

—*Carol Hopson*

Questions for Reflection and Obedience

1. Has God put someone on your heart that you need to reach out to?

2. What thoughts have kept you from ministering to the needs of this person or others? (If your life is busy with home responsibilities and children, you may not be able to take on an outside ministry. However, to take your focus off yourself, think of ways you can have a servant's heart without leaving your home . . . calls, notes, prayer, etc.)

3. How might helping someone else change your daily outlook?

4. Write down something that God has revealed to you through His Word or some area you've seen Him work in recently. Be prepared to share this with others so that your heart will turn to praise (Ps. 34:1).

~Day 5~
IS YOUR SHIELD IN PLACE?

Above all be sure you take faith as your shield, for it can quench every burning missile the enemy hurls at you. (Eph. 6:16 Phillips)

How do you prepare for your day? I'm sure you have some sort of routine including a shower, combing your hair, and putting on your clothes. It's so obvious to us to get our outer person ready for the day. I'm one of those who wouldn't think of going out without hair and makeup in place, and yet I've often gone out completely undressed spiritually.

Thinking I was prepared for my day because of my outward preparation, I have been sadly wounded by the burning missiles of the enemy. Matthew Henry states that these missiles are called "fiery darts because of their swift and undiscerned flight, and the deep wounds that they give to the soul." He goes on to explain that faith is the shield that renders these darts ineffectual. Therefore, if I have started my day without committing it into my Father's hands, including the unknown, the changed plans, the joys and pains, I'm unprepared for battle.

To get my shield of faith in place, I must read God's Word and claim a verse or thought from it each day. For example, Psalm 34:1 states, *I will bless the Lord at all times; His praise shall continually be in my mouth.* And verse 19 promises that *many are the afflictions of the righteous; but the Lord delivers him out of them all.* With this preparation, I can face any battle. When I'm met with changed plans or discouragement, I will praise God openly out of obedience. I will thank Him for deliverance before I know how He will accomplish it and thereby keep my shield in place. Because I'm not wallowing in doubt or worry, Satan has nothing to work with in my mind, and I can continue to live victoriously.

Is your shield in place today?

The Shield of Faith

Have you misplaced your shield today?
Did Satan strike a blow?
Did worry, fear, or doubt set in?
Just where did your faith go?

You've heard God's words; they're very clear,
"Stand firm; be on your guard,"
But having faith when under fire
is sometimes very hard.

Again God's loving, gentle voice
says, "Child, take up your shield,"
and once again you realize
that you forgot to yield.

So let's start out today anew
with shield of faith in place
and watch God give us victory
as each new day we face.

—*Carol Hopson*

Questions for Reflection and Obedience

1. Do you presently spend time getting your shield in place as a part of your morning routine?

2. If not, do you now see the importance of this part of your clothing?

3. Look back a few days, and write down what would have been different in certain circumstances if you had put your shield of faith in action. (Think of thoughts, actions, words.)

4. Look up the following Scriptures, and write down how obedience to these would shield you from the wounds of Satan's fiery darts:

   Galatians 5:19–25

   Ephesians 4:1–3, 29–32

   Colossians 3:8–17

~Day 6~
YOU'RE ONE DAY CLOSER!

If you are then raised up with Christ, reach out for the highest gifts of Heaven, where Christ reigns in power. Be concerned with the heavenly things, not with the passing things of earth. For, as far as this world is concerned, you are already dead, and your true life is a hidden one in God, through Christ. (Col. 3:1–3 Phillips)

It seems like everyone I love is in transition right now. They either need to move for various reasons, need to give up their dreams, or need to change their courses. When my husband and I were faced with a sudden move and unexpected change of plans, my thoughts were often pulled in the wrong direction. The *whys, what ifs,* and *if onlys* would plague me until I came in line with what Jesus would have me do.

As we were leaving our home that we loved, my parents, in their eighties, were also needing to leave their home and move to a smaller residence near family. Other loved ones were also leaving comfortable homes and making changes. As I asked the Lord for peace and power to face the changes and encourage others in the process, He had me focus on heaven. Isn't it amazing and sad how little we think of heaven until we get uncomfortable here on earth? We get so caught up in the temporal things that we enjoy, our homes, our children, our relationships. As long as everything is going well, we have no need to think of heaven.

Maybe that's why God allows us to go through difficult times so we will remember that this world is not our home. The early Christians often focused on heaven and all that awaited them because they knew this earthly home was only a temporary residence. **Sometimes we need to get a little homesick for heaven** (2 Peter 3:12–14).

Why not thank God right now for the joyful, comforting anticipation of heaven?

One Day Closer to Glory

One day closer to glory;
that's why my heart can sing!
For things on this earth are not lasting,
never to them should I cling.

Houses are only a framework
where love and contentment abide;
and wealth won't be needed in heaven
where someday real soon we'll reside.

So let's keep our focus on heaven
and all that eternity brings.
Together with all the beloved
and great hymns of praise we will sing.

No sickness, no heartache, no moving,
and never saying good-bye,
Oh, what a day of rejoicing
when Jesus appears in the sky!

We're one day closer to glory;
today other thoughts shall flee.
Tomorrow our Savior may take us
to live with Him eternally!

—*Carol Hopson*

Questions for Reflection and Obedience

1. Are you or someone you love going through a time of transition right now? Describe the transition.

2. How is this affecting you?

3. How are these emotions controlling your day? Explain how they are affecting your actions and reactions.

4. Read Psalm 42, and write down the words that describe David's emotions in his time of trouble. Then read Psalm 56, and write out the specific choices he made that brought him peace.

   David's emotions:

   David's choices:

~Day 7~
THE GOOD THING IS!

But the lovingkindness of the Lord is from everlasting to everlasting on those who fear Him, and His righteousness to children's children. (Ps. 103:17)

It was a terrible day, humanly speaking. I received a call that a friend's husband had committed suicide in their home. She found him just before her three children arrived home from junior high and high school. The shock for everyone was overwhelming! Many had been praying for this man's salvation for years. His wife and children were all believers, but to our knowledge, he had not given his heart to the Lord.

This dear wife and mother was one of those special servants of God who always saw the good in everyone and everything. She had truly been a light in the midst of her circumstances. One of the things she was known for was her phrase, "But the good thing is . . .," followed by some positive, encouraging words for whoever was listening.

Then at her husband's memorial service, she shared that the day her husband took his life was the first time that she couldn't think of what the "good thing" was. However, as over one thousand people listened intently to this precious servant of God, she shared how God was showing her what the "good things" were—the love and faith of her children, the incredible support of friends and church family, and the opportunity to proclaim her faith to everyone there. (Over one-half of those in attendance were unchurched.) It was a day I shall never forget.

Are you thanking God for the good things in your life today, or are you dwelling on negative things? God wants to use you this very day. Are you willing?

But the Good Thing Is!
(for my friend)

Dear God, I don't know what to think;
my life does not seem fair!
I hadn't planned on these events,
But the good thing is . . . You care!

My children have such heavy hearts
and may feel some despair.
Their father is not here for them,
But the good thing is . . . You're there!

I do not know what lies ahead
or how I will get through.
There're bills to pay, I don't know how,
But the good thing is . . . You do!

I will not think too far ahead
or walk through unknown doors.
I'll simply trust Your loving care
'Cause the good thing is . . . I'm Yours!

with my love,
Carol Hopson
November 9, 1998

Stand and see the salvation of the Lord on your behalf. . . .
Do not fear or be dismayed; for the Lord is with you.
(2 Chron. 20:17)

Questions for Reflection and Obedience

1. What are some "good things" in your life right now that often take a backseat to your problems? Write out as many as you can think of.

2. Read Psalm 103:1–12, and write out the "good things" God has done for you that you can rejoice about today.

3. Which one of these "good things" means the most to you and why?

4. Spend time in prayer, asking God to help you keep the "good things" in mind, especially when it's most difficult.

~Day 8~
CAN YOU KNOW GOD'S WILL?

I have been crucified with Christ; and it is no longer I who live, but Christ lives in me; and the life which I now live in the flesh I live by faith in the Son of God, who loved me, and delivered Himself up for me. (Gal. 2:20)

How often have you said, "I just wish I knew God's will." I hear it often as I meet with women at various conferences and retreats. "If God would just write me a letter!" they say to me. Well, guess what? He did! The Bible is His letter of love, encouragement, and instruction for our lives. So why are we often confused about what His will is?

In my own experience, when I'm unsure or confused, I am still hanging onto my desires in a given situation. Therefore, I cannot clearly see what God wants of me. The "I," which was *crucified with Christ,* is trying to take control.

It wasn't until I let go of living near my grandchildren that I clearly saw that God wanted me to move to another state in obedience to Him. The key to knowing God's will is to desire it above all else. My godly father has often said, "If you truly desire God's will, you're in it."

Search me O God, and know my heart; try me and know my anxious thoughts; and see if there be any hurtful way in me, and lead me in the everlasting way (Ps. 139:23–24). **Search your heart today and see if anything is keeping you from wholeheartedly accepting God's will, whatever it may be.** If you're still holding on to something, confess it, and ask God to help you be strong in your commitment. Then walk on in faith that God will make His will known to you when your heart is ready to obey.

In the Center of the Circle

In the center of the circle
of the will of God I stand!
I do not know what lies ahead
but trust it to His hand.

This morning I will praise Him
as I face this bright new day
and think of all He's given me
and from doubts turn away.

I cannot know what is in store,
my future is unknown.
But God has promised each of us
He dearly loves His own.

And He will show me just in time
His purpose and His plan,
as in the center of the circle
of His will I stand.

—*Carol Hopson*

Questions for Reflection and Obedience

1. In what area do you desire to know God's will today?

2. What has been your experience when you have asked God to show you His will in this area?

3. As you examine your heart and your desires, is there some plan or agenda you are still hanging on to? To know God's will, you have to honestly answer this question, and then lay it on the altar and trust His plan.

4. Psalm 37:3–9 will help you understand the steps needed to commit your circumstances to the Lord. List those steps below and then apply them to your situation.

~Day 9~
ARE YOU WAITING PATIENTLY?

I waited patiently for the Lord; and He inclined to me, and heard my cry. He brought me up out of the pit of destruction, out of the miry clay. (Ps. 40:1–2)

When our children were very small, we taught them to say, "This isn't my favorite" about foods or experiences they didn't like. We had heard too many children say, "I hate this!" and didn't want our children to be so ungrateful and impolite. To teach them this, there was a particular consequence they learned to avoid. If they came to the dinner table and said, "I hate carrots!" they were treated to a second serving of carrots. After only one or two slips, they never used the word *hate* again.

God's sense of humor and love seems to use the same strategy on me sometimes. Waiting is not my favorite thing. So I always try to find the shortest line in a store. Usually, it ends up being the slowest line, and I realize that God is teaching me again to be patient. Sometimes I feel the same way with waiting situations in my life. I think I know the shortest way to get to the desired end, but God doesn't usually see it the way I do. Therefore, I must wait patiently.

To wait patiently is to wait on God alone for the answer. To wait patiently is to not get frustrated, impatient, or angry when things don't go as quickly as I planned. To wait patiently is to trust that God's timing is best. **To wait patiently is to believe that God has a purpose in having me wait that will make me more Christlike.** *Wait for the Lord; be strong, and let your heart take courage; yes, wait for the Lord* (Ps. 27:14).

Wait Again?

Well, Lord, I'm here again
in this waiting spot.
It seems that learning patience
is my continual lot.

Isn't there an easier way?
Don't you understand
all I want is answers now?
I want to know Your plan.

Waiting, waiting, time lags on.
Why is it so tough?
Why is it that praying hard
isn't quite enough?

You say You want to teach me
more patience than before.
You say You want to use me
to new heights I must soar?

Change my heart, dear Jesus,
and may Your will be done.
Change my thoughts, my goals, my dreams
'Til Yours and mine are one.

—*Carol Hopson*

Questions for Reflection and Obedience

1. What is your typical attitude while you are waiting?

2. How does your attitude show patience or impatience with God's timing?

3. How can these verses encourage you while you are waiting: Proverbs 3:5–6; Psalm 56:9–11; James 4:10; 5:7–8?

4. How might you grow in your Christian experience because of this waiting situation you are facing?

~Day 10~
Are You Singing Today?

He put a new song in my mouth, a song of praise to our God;
many will see and fear, and will trust in the Lord. (Psalm 40:3)

I was listening to a dear friend share her life story. She had been through much pain and discouragement, but she had recently discovered the peace of casting her burdens on the Lord. As we shared our hearts over lunch, I could see the Scriptures come alive. I had personally witnessed the pit she had been in and how God had reached down and pulled her out of the pit of discouragement of trying to work things out by herself. Now it was evident that others were seeing the "new song" in her heart and were asking what had happened. What joy!

I, too, have experienced that same process. When my husband and I were going through the fire in a Christian organization, I was flung into a pit of despair. But as I looked to my Rescuer to bring me out of the pit, He rescued me and put my feet on the solid rock. The rock included the truths and promises of His Word which I needed to obey and claim as my own. Emotions could no longer control me if I was going to keep my feet on the rock. Then He gave me a new song to sing about victory even in the darkest night. Because of God's faithfulness, many have heard my song and have decided to trust God with their lives.

Are you in an emotional pit? Have you allowed God to rescue you (Ps. 40:2)? Is there a testimony in your heart that you are not singing? **Remember that praise gives purpose to the pit.** Practice praising your heavenly Father today to anyone you see—your family, friends, and neighbors. Psalm 40:3 might happen in your life this very day!

My New Song

At first I couldn't sing a note; no song was in my heart.
I felt betrayed, deserted, my life had come apart!

Satan saw my circumstance and recognized my pain
And thought, "Aha, a victory! Another 'saint' I'll claim!"

But knowing that the choice was mine to get my shield in place,
I ran to God and started in on facing fear with faith.

The pages of my journal saw God's truths come alive.
And I knew that my only hope was in Him to abide.

As I began this walk of faith, again not what I planned,
I saw how lovingly He came and took hold of my hand.

He guided me through unknown doors
and held me when I cried.
He helped me leave the hurt with Him and said,
"I'm on your side."

I don't know when my new song came or how it got its start.
I only know that gradually it flowed out from my heart.

I'll bless the Lord through all my times;
my days are in His hands.
And I will serve him faithfully, though not as I had planned.

For He is sovereign, He is God, the Potter . . . I'm the clay.
And I have found that true joy comes when I choose to obey.

So I sing because He's faithful, and I sing because I'm free,
For what my Father has in store is what is best for me.

—*Carol Hopson*

Questions for Reflection and Obedience

1. What kind of situations put you in a pit?

2. Do you feel that you are in an emotional pit right now? If yes, what emotions are you allowing to control your life?

3. List below some characteristics of Jesus our Rock that are meaningful to you. Use Scripture to support this (use Psalms 18 and 31).

4. According to Psalm 27:11; 42:11 and 56:11, what is missing when you allow your emotions to take you on an unstable path?

~Day 11~
HOW ABOUT SOME WEED PULLING?

When I kept silent about my sin, my body wasted away through my groaning all day long. For day and night Thy hand was heavy upon me; my vitality was drained away as with the fever heat of summer. I acknowledged my sin to Thee, and my iniquity I did not hide; I said, "I will confess my transgressions to the Lord"; and Thou didst forgive the guilt of my sin. (Psalm 32:3–5)

I love working in the garden! I enjoy planting flowers, watering them, trimming the blooms, and cutting stems for bouquets. I find such joy in the beauty God has created for our enjoyment. But there's one thing I don't enjoy—weed pulling. I usually let the weeds grow too long, and so the job is overwhelming. I'm discouraged before I even begin. If I could only be faithful to do a little weed pulling each day, my garden would be beautiful and much easier to maintain.

In my head, I know the same principle applies to my spiritual garden. I love growing in Christ, reading the Word, teaching, speaking, and encouraging others. But sometimes in the joy of those things, the spiritual weed pulling gets neglected or even ignored. What weeds might I need to pull?

- the weed of pride
- the weed of unkind thoughts
- the weed of grasping my rights
- the weed of bitterness
- the weed of busyness that doesn't allow for time alone with my heavenly Father

Confessing my sin is pulling the weeds and allowing God's beauty to grow in me again. The weed repellent of God's Word can then be applied to help protect from future growth. There can be no true beauty or peace in a spiritual garden that is overrun with weeds. **Do you need to get your gloves on and go to work?**

Weeds

Weeds, weeds,
always in my garden,
choking out the beauty of each row.

Weeds, weeds,
every day some new ones,
always seems that they much quicker grow.

Weeds, weeds,
creeping into my life,
choking out the beauty of His love.

Weeds, weeds,
need to be uprooted,
seeking God to cleanse me from above.

Weeds, weeds,
never need to be there
if my garden's daily in His care.

—*Carol Hopson*

Questions for Reflection and Obedience

1. Have you made a habit of spiritual weed pulling?

2. What weeds need to be uprooted right now?

   a. in your thought life:

   b. in your actions:

   c. in a specific relationship:

   d. in your relationship with your Lord:

3. Read Colossians 3 to help you pull the necessary weeds.
   Write out a verse that you want to focus on.

~Day 12~
ARE YOU CAPTURING YOUR THOUGHTS?

We are destroying speculations and every lofty thing raised up against the knowledge of God, and we are taking every thought captive to the obedience of Christ. (2 Cor. 10:5)

I was facing my first MRI, and the dreaded word *cancer* had been mentioned. Once it entered my mind, thoughts of every kind began to take over: *I'm too young to die! Will it be painful? How far has it spread?* These were not thoughts based on truth but on fear. I was jumping ahead to the worst conclusions and wasn't prepared to handle them. You see, when we are faced with a definite, difficult situation, God gives the grace to see us through (2 Cor. 10:9).

Isn't it amazing how often we jump ahead of God and expect the worst? We put ourselves through so much misery by trying to second-guess what is ahead, and usually we end up defeated and out of touch with God's will. That's because we haven't *captured our thoughts* in obedience to Christ. We have not *destroyed speculations* but speculate on everything and then wonder why we're so disheartened and discouraged.

To be obedient to 2 Corinthians 10:5, I had to check my thoughts continually and not let discouraging ones take root. I needed to thank God for His sufficient grace and rest in the future He had planned for me. And I needed to trust that He loved me and would take care of me. This meant leaving the results of the MRI in His hands and continuing to praise Him for His loving care.

Are you ready to destroy your worst speculations and obey God by capturing those negative thoughts before they take root? **Have you left the results of your situation in God's hands?**

The MRI

Well, Lord, I'm going in today to have an MRI.
It's not just what I wanted, but on You I will rely.

I've heard some awful things
about just being in that tube,
and if I didn't know Your peace,
I don't know what I'd do.

The time has come to lay right down
and put You to the test.
I'm doing what the doctor said;
now, Lord, please do the rest!

It's not so bad inside of here; it's clean and fresh and light
and not so very scary, but it is a little tight.

Now, Lord, I'm going to sing some songs,
not loud, but in my heart,
And keep my mind on praising You
each moment from the start.

It sounds like I'm inside a pipe
with someone banging loud,
but inside I prefer to think
I'm resting in a cloud.

Oh, no, dear Lord, I have to cough.
I'm not supposed to move.
So I am going to ask you, Lord,
the urge to cough remove!

I knew that you could do it, Lord;
the urge has gone away.
I didn't have to call for help,
just trust You and obey.

I wonder how long it has been since this ordeal began?
I've sung a lot and thought and prayed
and even a poem planned.

How timely that our Bible study
this week deals with stress,
and God is causing me to grow
by going through this test.

It just can't be.
What words of bliss, coming though little holes:
"It's over, Mrs. Hopson. You may get up and go."

Out I slide as smooth as glass on a conveyer belt.
The room seems large and spacious,
and I've never better felt.

What did I learn from all of this?
What lesson was in store?
That trusting God to calm my heart
brought peace and so much more.

I learned we have two choices
when faced with fear or stress.
We either choose to deny God's power
or in Him truly rest.

—*Carol Hopson*

Questions for Reflection and Obedience

1. How have you run ahead of God in your thought life?

2. What has this thinking produced?

3. Write down the negative thoughts you need to take captive today in obedience to Christ.

4. How will you use these Scriptures to change from negative thoughts to obedient, trusting thoughts?

   1 Peter 5:6–7

   James 1:2–7

   Philippians 4:6, 8

~Day 13~
ARE YOU THANKFUL FOR SMALL THINGS?

In everything give thanks; for this is God's will for you in Christ Jesus. (1 Thess. 5:18)

Did you know that thankfulness can restore peace to the heart? As I sat eating my breakfast this morning, the Lord reminded me of something. Eating seems like such a small thing, just a part of our daily routine, and yet a couple of years ago, I couldn't eat anything. For several months, a major infection invaded my body. I was reduced to surviving on Gatorade and fluids that entered my body intravenously. Each day I would tell the Lord that I'd never take eating for granted again and pray that I could keep even two bites of toast in me. The importance of eating became my primary thought each day.

After the infection was finally cured, I thanked God with my whole heart before each meal . . . for several months. Then gradually, I forgot what it was like to be unable to eat anything, and I again took this daily privilege for granted. It's amazing how we ask God to help us in a certain area. Then when He does, we forget to be thankful for more than a few days. The children of Israel were notorious for this. But I don't do very well myself. The Lord answers, and I'm thankful, then I'm on to the next crisis or petition.

The Lord tells us to bring our petitions to Him with gratitude (Phil. 4:6–7). This gratitude should be for what He has done in the past, what He will do in the future, and the small blessings of today. This builds a mental altar of God's faithfulness for us, and we can be at peace in our present circumstances because of His past record.

Will you thank Him for the small things today?

A Grateful Heart

My heart is brimming over
with the knowledge of Your love,
boundless, everlasting,
filled with blessings from above.

I cannot understand
the kind of love You've shown to me;
I'm so unworthy, undeserving,
selfish as can be.

And yet You go on loving
and forgiving o'er and o'er.
You never seem to hold a grudge
but love me all the more.

Help me to forgive like You
the ones that hurt me so.
Help me then to love like You
so through me Your love shows.

—*Carol Hopson*

Questions for Reflection and Obedience

1. List at least eight things for which you are grateful today:

2. Write down a specific answer to prayer in the past months, and thank God again. Add it to your mental *altar of thanksgiving* by thanking God each morning for that answer.

3. Stop now and thank God for His goodness and faithfulness to you today. To make it more real, write out your prayer.

4. Read through Psalm 56, then pray it in loving obedience to your heavenly Father.

~Day 14~
IT'S NEVER EASY!

For you have been called for this purpose, since Christ also suffered for you, leaving you an example for you to follow in His steps, who committed no sin, nor was any deceit found in His mouth; and while being reviled, He did not revile in return; while suffering, He uttered no threats, but kept entrusting Himself to Him who judges righteously. (1 Pet. 2:21–23)

Most of us have had one or more of those times. The phone rings, the message comes through, and your life changes forever. There have been many in my life: the death of someone I loved, news of cancer, a friend's broken cries.

When my husband and I moved to a ministry in the Pacific Northwest, it was in obedience to the Lord. We left family, a ministry we began fifteen years earlier, friends, Bible studies we led, and a wealth of memories. We settled into our new lives, the ministry flourished, and we put down roots. We rejoiced in God's ability to give us joy in this new place without all the people and ministries we dearly loved.

Then suddenly, in one phone call, my husband's job ended without warning after just two short years. My heart was broken . . . again! My human reactions ranged from anger to self-pity to bitterness. But after a few hours of weeping and praying, the Lord brought His precious Word to mind and helped me keep His promises in focus (Prov. 3:5–6)

I began a "Facing Fear with Faith" journal and decided to take God completely at His word. For each anger or fear I faced, God met me with His Word. For instance, I would cry out, "Why did this happen?" and the Lord would respond with, *Do not lean on your own understanding.* When I shouted, "It's just not fair!" God reminded me through His Word to trust myself and my husband to *Him who judges righteously.* When I acknowledged that God was still God, and I listened to His words instead of my own, He calmed my heart and restored my peace.

The road is never easy, **but God always provides a way.**

This Isn't Easy, Lord!

This isn't very easy, Lord;
It's not what I had planned.
The situation I now face
seems to have hit the fan!

The load is getting heavy,
And my heart is filled with pain.
I need Your loving comfort
to heal my soul again.

It seems so difficult to trust
when all around grows dark.
But if I don't accept Your will,
I've truly missed the mark.

For You have said, "Be not afraid!
The battle is not yours."
And I must willingly obey
and through this trial endure.

I *will* decide to heed Your voice
and trust You with my pain.
I *will* take up my shield of faith
and in Your Word remain.

I cannot see why this must be
with human eyes of mine.
But I *will* leave it at Your feet
And praise You ahead of time.

—*Carol Hopson*

Questions for Reflection and Obedience

1. What is your first reaction to a difficult phone call or a disheartening situation?

2. Do you think that reaction reflects trust in a sovereign, loving God? Why or why not?

3. In 1 Peter 2:21–23, Paul says we are to follow Jesus' example when suffering. List the ways we are to be obedient in these verses. Then seek God's help in making them active and evident in your life.

   a.

   b.

   c.

   d.

   e.

~Day 15~
WHAT KIND OF TROPHY ARE YOU?

And God is able to make all grace abound to you, that always having all sufficiency in everything, you may have an abundance for every good deed. (2 Cor. 9:8)

It made no sense to me. My dear friend's husband had been diagnosed with a rare disease for which there was no cure. He is a strong, godly man who loves life, loves his family, and loves the Lord with all his heart.

"Why do these things happen?" I'm often asked. And I usually reply, "Only God knows." He sees the big picture, but we see only our small portion with our limited sight. What I do know is that each trial God allows in our journey is an opportunity for growth or despair. Just as an athlete receives a trophy after winning a race, we become living trophies on display for the world to see as we go through life's crisis. The question is, what kind of trophies will we be:

- trophies of bitterness?
- trophies of anger?
- trophies of discontent?
- trophies of pride?
- or trophies of God's grace?

To me, to have God's grace on display in my life has become my goal. In love, He has allowed me to be His servant on display—a trophy of His all-sufficient grace when I choose to be obedient. I've seen my dear friends be trophies of unwavering trust in the midst of tremendous pain and unknown futures. I'm encouraged at how brightly they, as a trophies of unending faith in God, are shining.

How would others title your life's trophy so far?

What Kind of Trophy?

What kind of trophy am I?

Do I take time to show . . .
that I care
that I love
that I encourage?

Do I shine as a light . . .
when it's painful
when it's unfair
when it's inconvenient?

Do I reflect my Savior . . .
with a forgiving heart
with a selfless mind
with total acceptance?

—*Carol Hopson*

Questions for Reflection and Obedience

1. What would your family say you are a trophy of?

2. Does that make you happy or sad? What would you like to be a trophy of?

3. How do you desire for God to be glorified through your life?

4. How do you need to recognize God's sufficiency in your life? Read 2 Corinthians 9:8 again, and write down how it applies to your situation.

~*Day* 16~
IS YOUR DADDY THERE?

Do not fear, for I am with you; do not anxiously look about you, for I am your God. I will strengthen you, surely I will help you, surely I will uphold you with My righteous right hand. (Isa. 41:10)

As a child, I always looked forward to summer vacations when our family would take our annual camping trip. I loved being out in the woods, hiking, fishing, cooking outside, and having fun family times around the campfire each night. I also remember several occasions when a bear would find our camp interesting and decide to investigate. Once he sniffed right up against the tent I was sleeping in, and another time he shook the tiny trailer I was sleeping in as he searched for food. I also have great memories of forging across ice-cold, rushing streams to get to a perfect spot for fishing or a picnic. Were these scary situations to me? Not really. I remember them as fun and exciting. Do you know why? My daddy was there. I knew he would protect me and give his life, if necessary, for my safety because he loved me that much. **The knowledge of my father's presence changed everything.**

How often we lose sight of our heavenly Father's presence. At first, we take it for granted, then we forget He's even with us when fearful situations arise. It must pain Him to see us carrying burdens of fear and worry when He gave His Son's life so that we could have peace in the midst of trials (1 Pet. 4:12–13).

When we're fearful, we either don't trust God to take care of us, or we've forgotten His promise to never leave us or forsake us (Heb. 13:5). Both are a slap in His holy face.

73

We need to ask forgiveness and then ask for help in staying aware of His presence and power in our lives.

He gave everything for you. Can't you trust Him with your life?

Peace

Peace, what is it?
Some ethereal feeling . . .
Is it freedom from cares and hurts and scars?
Is it wounds that don't need healing?

Peace, what is it?
A jovial, trivial smile . . .
Is it never needing to shed a tear?
Is it happiness all the while?

Peace, what is it?
A strength we can't understand . . .
It's living and feeling and knowing
That God has hold of your hand!

—*Carol Hopson*

Questions for Reflection and Obedience

1. What traits of your earthly father give you comfort?

2. If you could not think of positive traits, or if you don't know your father, describe five traits that you would most like to have in a father:

3. Do you realize that your heavenly Father has all the wonderful characteristics that you would desire in an earthly father and more? Practice thanking Him for who He really is.

4. Read Psalm 91, and describe the security we have in the Lord.

~Day 17~
GOD IS IN CONTROL!

My purpose will be established, and I will accomplish all My good pleasure. . . . Truly I have spoken; truly I will bring it to pass. I have planned it, surely I will do it. (Isa. 46:10–11)

Susie was my college roommate, my best friend, and ultimately, my sister-in-law. She was a ray of sunshine that couldn't be squelched. When Susie gave her life to the Lord as a late teenager, she gave her all. From that point on, she trusted God completely. Though she had not been raised in a Christian home, she truly fell in love when she met Jesus and never turned back. This love and trust carried her through the deaths of her mother, her father, and her only sister—all cancer victims. A lot to handle? You bet, but that's not all. You see, Susie too had cancer for the last fifteen years of her life. She suffered through many surgeries, chemotherapy treatments, hair losses, and great pain. Yet Susie never complained. Never!

She would always share that God knew what He was doing, and He was in control. And she never lost her enthusiasm for life and her radiant personality. Do you want to know why? She truly fell in love with Jesus, realizing what He had done for her. The love and commitment she had outweighed her human emotions and desires. The night she died, she awoke from a coma just long enough to say to all her family gathered around her bed, "God is in control!"

Susie's life touched doctors, nurses, cancer patients, numerous churches, family, friends, and me. Because of her faithfulness, many learned to trust in the Lord. I knew that, because of her peace, God could see me through anything. Thank You, God, for the gift of Susie.

Does your love for God outweigh your fears?

God Is in Control!

You may not *feel* it every day
as disappointments come.
You might be quite discouraged
and only want to run.

You may not *see* it with your eyes
as problems seem to mount.
And you might feel you're all alone
and your life doesn't count.

You may not *think* there's any hope
for happiness and peace.
You think that it's impossible
for fears and doubts to cease.

You may not *feel*, you may not *see*,
your *thought life's* at a low.
But peace will come when you agree
that *God is in control!*

—*Carol Hopson*

Questions for Reflection and Obedience

1. How much do you love the Lord? Write out your feelings.

2. What would you not give up for Him?

3. Read Jeremiah 17:5–6, and write out what happens to someone who trusts only himself to handle things.

4. According to Jeremiah 17:7–8, what is promised for the person who trusts that God is in control?

~Day 18~
ARE YOU TIRED TODAY?

Come to me, all of you who are weary and over-burdened, and I will give you rest! Put on my yoke and learn from me. For I am gentle and humble in heart and you will find rest for your souls. For my yoke is easy and my burden is light. (Matt. 11:28 Phillips)

Are you tired of carrying the load that weighs you down? For two years of my childhood, I carried a cello to elementary school. What a relief when friends would see me walking and offer me a ride to school. It was such a great feeling to put my load into their car and feel free of my burden.

I didn't always have a choice then, but I do now. Jesus says to come to Him if we are weary and overburdened. I can surely identify with that, can't you? At times I've allowed a problem to weigh me down so much that my peace and joy have vanished, and I want someone else to carry the load for a while.

What relief does Jesus offer—a yoke? What is freeing about a yoke? He asks us to willingly "take" His yoke on us and learn from Him. When oxen were yoked together, there was a leader and a follower. As long as one followed the leader, all was well. But if the two tried to go in different directions, there was trouble.

To get relief from my burdens, I need to submit to the yoke of His leadership, willingly go with His plan without fighting against it. Then I don't have to worry about trying to control and fix everything. And I'm free to learn what He wants me to learn, to have *a gentle and humble spirit.* This *being yoked* to my Savior will ultimately bring rest to my weary soul.

Are you chafing at the yoke or submitting to it? Remember, He wants to lighten your load.

The Yoke of Rest

Take My yoke upon you,
and I will give you rest.
Give Me all your burdens,
and I'll give you My best.

Why do we distrust this
and all our burdens bear?
Why do we still worry
and think God doesn't care?

Because we haven't trusted
His sovereignty above.
And we have not submitted to
His gentle yoke of love.

We look at all around us
and discontent sets in.
We do not claim His promises,
and our hearts fill with sin.

Confession is the first step
to finding rest and peace.
Then gladly take His yoke of love
and all your cares release.

Then God will do abundantly
more than words can say.
He'll give you His sufficient grace
for resting every day!

—*Carol Hopson*

Questions for Reflection and Obedience

1. What are you most tired of in your daily struggle?

   too much activity

2. Do you feel all alone in this? Read Isaiah 40:28–31 and Isaiah 41:10, and write what the Lord has promised you.

3. What do you need to do to be willingly yoked with Christ? What decisions do you need to make today?

   yield
   courage
   job

4. If you recognize where you've been pulling against His yoke, write it down and confess it now so you can be at rest.

   not my will but yours, Lord

   His way his schedule

~Day 19~
HAVE YOU FOUND CONTENTMENT?

Not that I speak from want; for I have learned to be content in whatever circumstance I am. I know how to get along with humble means, and I also know how to live in prosperity; in any and every circumstance I have learned the secret of being filled and going hungry, both of having abundance and suffering need. I can do all things through Him who strengthens me. (Phil. 4:11–13)

I've asked many people what they think they would need to make them content. Here are some of their answers: enough money to pay bills with a little left over, a bigger house, a more loving spouse or children, knowledge of the future, and answers to all their problems.

Sounds pretty good, doesn't it? Yet I remember talking to a friend on his fortieth birthday. He had more money than he could ever spend, the largest home in town, a loving wife, and from others' perspectives, a carefree life. As we visited and recalled our childhood and early years in the church youth group, his eyes filled with tears. "I've tried to get everything I thought would make me happy, and I've succeeded in the 'getting' part," he said. "But I'm less content than I've ever been."

So if money, fulfilled dreams, and success don't bring contentment, where can it be found? The secret is not in getting but in being! Paul learned to be content (or accept as from God any circumstance he was in) and find purpose in it. You see, we were created to serve and glorify God, and that is how we are satisfied. Paul's single desire was for Christ to use him and live through him. Therefore, he was always content with his situation (2 Cor. 12:9–10).

When we are not content, we have become double-minded. We want to please God and get our own way. It doesn't work.

Are you willing to be single-minded?

Where Contentment Lies

It isn't to be found in friends
who shower you with love,
For their love isn't lasting
like the Father's up above.

It isn't found in treasures rare
that worldly wealth can buy,
For those will not be worth a thing
when raptured in the sky.

It isn't to be found in things
that bring you lustful pleasure,
For what you sow you also reap—
a crop for God to measure.

It isn't found in titles grand
of which you boast right now,
For names will quickly fade away
when at His feet you bow.

If it's not found in all of these,
where will contentment lie?
In making Jesus Lord of all
'til His return is nigh.

—*Carol Hopson*

Questions for Reflection and Obedience

1. What have you honestly said you would need to make you content?

2. How has this changed over the past five years?

3. How does 1 Timothy 6:6–12 speak to you about contentment?

4. Write down two important warnings and two important commands found in these verses:

   Warnings:

   Commands:

~Day 20~
WHAT MATTERS TO GOD?

For it is by grace that you are saved, through faith. This does not depend on anything you have achieved, it is the free gift of God; and because it is not earned no man can boast about it. For God has made us what we are, created in Christ Jesus to do those good deeds which he planned for us to do. (Eph. 2:9–10 Phillips)

When you awoke this morning, was your first thought, "I wonder what matters to God today?" Probably not. Mine doesn't usually begin there either, but it should. Whether I'm cleaning, shopping, speaking, writing, counseling, or playing with my grandchildren, I should be controlled by doing, thinking, and saying what would please the Lord, not what feels good at the moment. If I truly believe that I am *"created in Christ Jesus to do those good deeds which he planned,"* I'll desire to allow His plan to flow through me to others throughout my daily walk.

When I had just moved to Seattle, I left my home for a local coffee shop to enjoy a latte on a dark, rainy, lonely day. As I sat there feeling a little sorry for myself, I asked God how He could use me right where I was. I looked at the server who seemed quite distraught, and when she had a moment, I asked if I could help her in any way. I said, "I'm a good listener." She let out a heart-wrenching statement, and I said, "I'll wait until you have a break if you'd like someone to talk to." In twenty minutes she joined me, and I could see she was in desperate need of God's love. She was ready and responsive, and the Lord met her need right there in the coffee shop.

What mattered to me originally as I went for a latte was finding some small pleasure on a dark, rainy day. **What mattered to God was that I be aware and available for His love to touch a soul for eternity.**

Are you willing to set your struggles aside and live this day with God's purpose in mind?

What Matters to God?

Have you ever stopped to think for awhile
what meeting the Lord will be like?
What will you think of when His face you see?
It could even happen tonight!

Will you tell Him about the degrees you acquired
through hard work and many long years?
Will you boast of your home and the things that you own
that bring you such stress and such fear?

Maybe you'll tell Him you wore the right clothes
from Nordstrom with labels to show,
that you bought the best that money could buy
and wanted your neighbors to know.

Or maybe you'll try to explain to the Lord
how busy you were with your plans,
and how doing His work just didn't quite fit,
so back to your comfort you ran.

These things will not matter when His face you see.
It's what has been done in His name.
Will there be stars in your crown of life?
Or will choices you made bring you shame?

What matters to Him is a heart that is set
on doing His will above all
by loving, forgiving, and praising His name
and always obeying His call.

It has to begin with a choice that you make
to please Him and not yourself.
For all you've collected materially
will someday be left on a shelf.

—*Carol Hopson*

Questions for Reflection and Obedience

1. What do you think God would say matters the most to Him in your day today?

   a. as a child of His:

   b. as a wife:

   c. as a mother:

   d. as a friend:

2. Which area is God speaking to you about right now?

3. Read 1 Corinthians 13, and write down one thing that matters to God that you will apply to your specific area of need.

~Day 21~
WHAT VOICE DO YOU LISTEN TO?

I am the good shepherd; and I know My own, and My own know Me. . . . My sheep hear My voice, and I know them, and they follow Me. (John 10:14, 27)

I've always heard that sheep are dumb animals, and as I watched them on my grandfather's farm, I could easily agree. However, there's one area in which they can be a great example to us. Did you know that they are never fooled by another shepherd's voice? Many shepherds can give the exact same call, but the sheep's ears will only perk up when he hears his own shepherd's voice. He will not move or respond to any other voice. If only my spiritual ears were that well trained.

A sheep responds this way because he knows this is the voice of the one who brings food, provides shelter and comfort, protects, heals, and gives love. You and I should know the same things about our Great Shepherd, but we don't always respond with obedience and single-mindedness. We've allowed too many other voices to cloud our minds. Instead of listening to our Shepherd's voice through reading His Word and prayer, we open our ears to man's ideas, our own self-motivated thoughts, and the world's distorted views. Then we find out there's no comfort or peace because we're in the wrong fold!

Is there another voice you've been listening to? The remedy for this is to study the Bible, listen intently to His words, and know the Shepherd's voice. Then follow His instructions, and stay as close to Him as possible for nourishment, safety, and comfort.

See to it that no one takes you captive through philosophy and empty deception, according to the tradition of men. (Col. 2:8)

His Voice

His voice . . .
tender, caring, loving, healing.
Do I know it?

His voice . . .
calling, reaching, warning, reproving.
Do I hear it?

His voice . . .
encouraging, uplifting, comforting, protecting.
Do I feel it?

His voice . . .
through others, His Word, in quietness and prayer.
Do I listen . . .
in silence . . .
in stillness . . .
in submission?

—*Carol Hopson*

Questions for Reflection and Obedience

1. What distracts you from hearing the Shepherd's voice?

2. How could you begin each day so that you would listen only to your Shepherd's voice?

3. What does your Shepherd say to do in the following passages?

   James 1:2–3:

   James 1:5–6:

   James 1:12:

   James 1:19–20:

   James 1:22–23:

~Day 22~
HOW ABOUT A NEW POINT OF VIEW?

*I pray that the eyes of your heart may be enlightened, so
that you may know what is the hope of His calling, what
are the riches of the glory of His inheritance in the saints,
and what is the surpassing greatness of His power toward
us who believe.* (Eph. 1:18–19)

As I sit in the San Diego airport again, waiting for my plane
to leave, I'm struck with the differing perspectives I can have
on yet another trip. One perspective is that I am leaving the
sunshine, leaving my husband, leaving my home and comfortable bed, leaving the freedom of having time to myself,
spending hours on an uncomfortable airplane, and spending
the weekend with people I've never met. It could sound quite
discouraging, tiring, and inconvenient. Sometimes it is.

However, God in His mercy has taught me a new way to
see things. From a godly perspective, I have numerous unknown opportunities ahead. I have the privilege of teaching God's Word five times this weekend to hungry, receptive
hearts. Then there's the great joy of meeting with individual
women who are burned out, heartbroken, or searching for
peace, and bringing them all that Jesus offers them. There's
the privilege of making new friends and the unmatched joy
of being obedient to God's call on my life to share Him and
His Word wherever and whenever I can.

Now, which perspective is most productive? Of course,
the second one is! Why would I even think about the nega-
tives? Because I'm human and have human weaknesses that
Satan loves to work on. So, I must be alert and on guard for
destructive, discouraging thoughts which rob me of my
peace, and choose the godly point of view.

Do you need to change your point of view?

It's Your Choice!

Another disappointment,
another change of plans,
Another day of unrest
and wringing of my hands.

Another promise broken,
another day of pain,
Another lonely outlook
in which I will remain.

or . . .

Another chance to praise Him
for what I cannot see.
Another chance to trust Him
to set my spirit free.

Another chance to open
my heart to do His will.
Another chance to follow
and show I trust Him still.

Another day to reach out
and meet another's need.
Another day to serve Him
and let Him work through me.

—*Carol Hopson*

Questions for Reflection and Obedience

1. Identify a wrong point of view you are holding on to.

2. Write out what God's point of view might be. Use 1 Peter 1:6–7; 4:12–19; and 5:5–7 to answer this.

3. Thank God ahead of time for what He might want to do in your life through this situation. Then pray for right thinking as you face each day.

~Day 23~
TRUST WHEN YOU CAN'T UNDERSTAND!

*And we know that God causes all things to work together
for good to those who love God, to those who are called
according to His purpose. (Rom. 8:28)*

Today I saw a remarkable thing. The bulbs I planted a
few months ago opened into gorgeous, colorful flowers.
How did that happen? I really don't understand it. I took
ugly bulbs and put them into dark, dirty places, and something beautiful, even extraordinary grew out of them. How
I enjoy the beauty that came from the darkness. The same
is true of ugly rocks or lumps of clay. Because of intense
pressure or difficult circumstances over time, they turn into
brilliant gems.

Again, I know the truth of it, but it doesn't make sense
to me. Do things have to be understandable to be accept-
able to me? *"For My thoughts are not your thoughts, neither
are your ways My ways," declares the Lord* (Isa. 55:8). And
Proverbs 3:5–6 warns us not to lean on our own understanding of things.

To say I must understand what God is doing in my life,
my marriage, my children's lives, my future is to minimize
God. It's saying that I need to know what God knows, and
that is not consistent with Scripture. He is the potter, I am
the clay. It is our faith that something good will come out
of the darkness that pleases our Lord. Our goal each day
should be threefold:

1. Keep believing God's promises and praising Him openly
   (Ps. 34:1).

2. Keep reading His Word for nourishment, endurance, and comfort (Ps. 119:28, 66, 129–130).
3. Keep allowing Him to bring forth fruit in the midst of our darkness (Jer. 17:7–8).

By being obedient in these things, we can bring joy to our heavenly Father and peace to our hurting souls.

The Other Side

God is weaving day by day
a pattern full of color,
full of twists and turns galore . . .
that doesn't match another.

It may look like a big mistake
when glancing at it here,
with knots and loose ends dangling . . .
making patterns quite unclear.

Sometimes hopeless it may seem,
because it doesn't fit
with what you thought 'twas all about . . .
and what your life would knit.

But sovereign God designs your days
when in Him you abide.
And someday when you see His face . . .
You'll see the other side.

—*Carol Hopson*

Questions for Reflection and Obedience

1. What promises of God are you not believing today because you don't understand what He's doing?

2. Write out your favorite verses that encourage you to trust God.

3. Read Psalm 19:7–14, and write out the benefits of God's Word to you right now.

4. Write out verses 13 and 14 in your own words, and make them a prayer of commitment to the Lord today.

~Day 24~
Are You Yelling or Listening?

Listen to Me, you stubborn-minded, who are far from righteousness. I bring near My righteousness, it is not far off; and My salvation will not delay. (Isa. 46:12–13)

I'm not used to being yelled at. I had pulled into a parking place that I had patiently been waiting for. After the driver backed out, I began to pull into the vacated space. As I was halfway in, a car screeched around the corner of the parking lot while a lady laid on the horn, opened her window, and treated me to a variety of words not meant for human ears. As my heart pounded, I opened my window and tried to tell her I'd back out and give her the space if she'd give me room. However, her verbal onslaught continued, and she couldn't hear a word I was saying. She then sped off and drove several rows away.

I got out of my car but couldn't carry on with my errands until I found her. You see, I wanted her to know that to me the parking place wasn't worth the confrontation. So I walked up and down until I saw her walking towards me. As she approached with fury in her eyes, I quickly said, "I'm so sorry I offended you. I didn't see you, or I would have gladly given you the parking spot. That's what I was trying to tell you. Please forgive me." She was speechless! She opened her mouth, but nothing came out. She just stared in unbelief.

After feeling I had done what I could to bring peace, I went on to the grocery store. As I was trying to disengage a stubborn grocery cart, someone behind me said, "Oh, please, let me help you!" The speechless woman I left in the parking lot had found her tongue.

How much of God's love and direction have we missed because we're too busy arguing our point or defending our rights? When we're shouting our displeasure at Him by our bitterness, anger, or disobedience, we're not able to hear His voice reminding us, *Did I not say to you, if you believe, you will see the glory of God?* (John 11:40).

Can You Use Me?

Can I help a friend, dear Lord?
Does someone have a need?
Maybe I could share a word,
A smile, a hug, a deed.

Can you use my hands, dear Lord,
To give a gentle touch?
Sometimes a willing, helping hand
Can mean so very much.

Can you use my voice, oh Lord?
Does someone need to hear
That there is One who sees her hurt
And knows her deepest fear?

Can you use my life, dear Lord?
Your servant I will be,
For leading others to the cross
Is what means most to me.

—*Carol Hopson*

Questions for Reflections and Obedience

1. Have you been yelling at God rather than listening? Explain how.

2. What is your first wrong reaction that closes your ears and opens your mind to what Satan wants you to do?

3. Will you confess your anger and listen now? Write out your prayer of confession.

4. To practice listening . . .

   a. Go to God first before you allow any emotional response.

   b. Read or recall a favorite portion of Scripture, and meditate on it.

   c. Ask yourself what Jesus would say or do in this situation.

   d. Pray, then obey!

~Day 25~
DID YOU LET THE THIEF IN?

Now may the Lord of peace Himself continually grant you peace in every circumstance. The Lord be with you all!
(Thess. 3:16)

Pursue peace with all men, and the sanctification without which no one will see the Lord. See to it that no one comes short of the grace of God; that no root of bitterness springing up causes trouble, and by it many be defiled.
(Heb. 12:14–15)

There have been many times in my life when I have allowed someone to rob me. And it's often happened while I was present. I'll bet you've done the same thing. Your day was going along just fine, you even had great morning devotions, and then it happened. A thief came in—someone who's negative, bitter, that difficult child, relative, or friend—and stole your joy and peace. It can be so frustrating, but did you realize that you unlocked the door and let it happen?

No person can rob me of peace unless I allow him or her to. If I allow God to stay in control of my thoughts, speech, and actions, the door will be bolted shut. This takes a conscious decision of my will to remain calm and peaceful and seek God's help while that difficult person is around or to remain focused on the truths of God's promises rather than on the phantoms of the mind.

Here are a few practical ways to bolt the door:

1. Begin your day thanking God for things He has blessed you with (Col. 3:17).

2. Before getting out of bed, ask God to help you live this day to please Him and to accept whatever He puts into it or takes out of it (Gal. 2:20).

3. Pray for a patient and forbearing spirit today (Col. 3:12–13).

4. Ask God to miraculously guard your thoughts and words (Ps. 34:1).

5. Thank Him for being faithful, and expect Him to answer your prayers (Ps. 138:8).

Bolt the Door!

Satan's tricks are all about.
Bolt the door; kick him out!

He sneaks inside your heart and mind
to see what doubts and fears he'll find.

And when he finds you're not in prayer,
he knows you're weak and sets a snare.

And if he sees your heart rejoice
because you've listened to God's voice,

he'll send a thought and bring some doubt
'cause that's what he is all about.

So bolt the door; kick him out!
Yes, Satan's tricks are all about,

But God is greater; He's the King,
so move doubts out and start to sing!

—*Carol Hopson*

Questions for Reflection and Obedience

1. Do you start each day recognizing that God is in control and wants to help you handle everything? Why or why not?

2. Who or what opens the door to your mind and robs your peace?

3. Are you able to see the thief before you choose to open the door? Explain how it happens.

4. What can you do to change how you respond to certain people, situations, or actions? (Use Hebrews 12:1–3 and James 1:19–22, 26.)

~Day 26~
Are You Bringing Joy to Your Father?

Or do you not know that your body is a temple of the Holy Spirit who is in you, whom you have from God, and that you are not your own? For you have been bought with a price: therefore glorify God in your body. (1 Cor. 6:19–20)

While strolling through a beautiful shopping mall near where we live, my husband and I were enchanted with a new fountain that adorned the center of the mall. It had been in progress for a long time, and I couldn't imagine why it would take almost a year to build just one fountain. As we watched it, we could see that it was different from anything we had ever seen before. The water did things we couldn't believe water could do, and we were entranced for fifteen minutes without taking our eyes off it.

In the corner of my vision, I noticed a young man, probably in his twenties, watching for as long as we were. I finally went over and asked him if he was as fascinated with it as we were. He smiled and said, "It's great to see it working the way it was designed to." As I questioned him further, he humbly admitted that he had designed and built it, and it was the first of its kind. "The real joy is seeing it do exactly what I created it to do," he commented.

As my husband and I drove home that day, I thought of my heavenly Father. He too designs our lives with great care and great love and is eager to see us fulfilling our purpose. But to truly bring joy to my Creator, I need to do exactly what I was created to do, to glorify Him where He has planted me. It's when I try to struggle through my pain and fears on my own that I lose my peace and feel like a victim. If I'm bitter, angry, or resentful, I'm not available to be used as I was created, and frustration sets in.

Could you be fighting against your Maker's plan today?

Will My Father Rejoice?

Created by my Father
to carry out His plan,
to show the world He loves them,
while guided by His hand.

Sometimes I seem to lose it
when self gets in the way,
and I forget my purpose
and choose to go astray.

It seems that I get all caught up
in such worldly ideals
and think that doing my own thing
has such a strong appeal.

Then God, in love, reminds me
through thoughts, His Word, and prayer
that His Son paid the price for me,
a gift beyond compare.

So as I change my attitude
and listen to His voice,
my heart will choose His plan so that
my Father will rejoice!

—*Carol Hopson*

Questions for Reflection and Obedience

1. According to Ephesians 2:8–10, why were you created?

2. What does the world tell you your purpose in life is, and how does it differ with what God says?

3. What could God want to do in and through you right now as you are in your own difficult circumstances?

   a.

   b.

   c.

~Day 27~
Does My Attitude Matter?

You're here to be light, bringing out the God-colors in the world. God is not a secret to be kept. We're going public with this, as public as a city on a hill. If I make you light-bearers, you don't think I'm going to hide you under a bucket, do you? I'm putting you on a light stand—shine! (Matt. 5:14–16 The Message)

I sat in the Mexican restaurant where I regularly met a friend. It was a time of growing and sharing that we both enjoyed and looked forward to. I usually arrived first and would try to get to know a waiter, a busboy, or even the cook, who came out to deliver food occasionally. On this day, I was giving my friend a copy of my new book *But God, I'm Tired of Waiting!* when the waiter walked up. My friend mentioned that I wrote the book and another one called *But God, This Wasn't My Plan!*

The waiter's response took me completely by surprise. He remarked, "If this lady wrote it, I want to read it." He went on to be appreciative of someone who had cared about him.

Did I know he was watching me? No, but I do know that God's purpose is for me to make the most of every opportunity (Eph. 5:16). It is also His plan for me to let His light shine through me wherever I am. You might think that's too difficult, but God never requires something of us without enabling us to do it. It also gives us a new perspective and makes each day exciting and purposeful. How dare we get so sidetracked with our own thoughts and agenda that we don't have time to allow Jesus to love others through us.

Are you sidetracked today? Are you available for the Lord to use right now in your particular circumstances? It may be your greatest opportunity to shine. **Remember, peace comes when we choose to live in obedience.**

Does It Really Matter?

Does it really matter what I do and what I say?
Do I always have to guard my words
and actions every day?

I just don't think I want to be a leader, not right now,
'Cause then I can't complain and question
You on why and how.

I'd like at least a day or two to feel a little bitter.
Or maybe I could try out what
It's like to be a quitter.

I wonder what it feels like to just sit and sulk awhile
And let those unkind thoughts continue
mile after mile?

But I can't seem to find a verse to let me go this route.
So, I'll just need to trust you, Lord,
to work this whole thing out!

—*Carol Hopson*

Questions for Reflection and Obedience

1. Are you usually aware that God's purpose is for you to be a light? What keeps you from being aware of this?

2. What would others observe in you that would drive them to Jesus? (Be very specific if you can—a warm smile, a friendly hello, patience)

   in a restaurant:

   in a grocery line:

   in your business or church meetings:

   in a family gathering:

   in a disagreement:

3. If these are disturbing questions for you, why not ask God right now to change your heart and mind so you're more aware of John 5:14–16?

~Day 28~
DO YOU HAVE AN IDOL?

Thus says the Lord, the King of Israel and his Redeemer,
the Lord of hosts: "I am the first and I am the last, and there
is no God besides Me." (Isa. 44:6)

While reading chapter 44 of Isaiah, the Lord opened
my eyes to some things that can easily become idols in my
life. Yes, I love the Lord and have dedicated my life to serve
Him, but I am not immune from erecting idols. It saddens
my heart to realize how easily it happens. Even the search
for a job for my husband became an idol for a short time. It
consumed my thoughts and took me away from God's purpose for my days.

We all know that money, power, and possessions can
become our idols as we spend all our time, thoughts, and
resources acquiring them. But I believe that wayward loved
ones can even become idols. We can get so sidetracked by
focusing on them, their problems, and what God or they
need to do. **Our problem is that we have misplaced our
passion.** It is one thing to pray diligently for a loved one
and then leave him or her in God's almighty hands. It be-
comes an idol when it consumes us with worry or doubt
and we give the situation all our time and energy. Can you
see how that robs our Lord of the time we should be spending in worship, in service, in praise, in gratitude, in asking
Him to touch others through us? No wonder God's words
are so clear to us.

You shall have no other gods before Me. . . . You shall not
worship them or serve them; for I, the Lord your God, am a
jealous God (Exod. 20:3, 5).

In All My Times

I love You, Lord!

in joyous times
in laughing times
in rewarding times
in loving and victorious times . . .

They're part of Your plan for me
because You love me.

I love You, Lord!

in difficult times
in hurtful times
in misunderstood times
in confusing and unfruitful times . . .

They're part of Your plan for me
because You love me!

—*Carol Hopson*

Questions for Reflection and Obedience

1. Has your situation or loved one become an "idol" in your life?

2. How much of your day and thought life is spent dwelling on this?

3. Read the following from God's Word, and write out how God desires to help you in your thought life:

   Proverbs 3:5–6

   Psalm 31:14–15

   Psalm 32:10–11

   Psalm 37:3–7

~Day 29~
YOU'RE VERY SPECIAL!

O Lord, Thou hast searched me and known me. Thou dost know when I sit down and when I rise up; Thou dost understand my thought from afar. Thou dost scrutinize my path and my lying down, and art intimately acquainted with all my ways. (Ps. 139:1–3)

I will instruct you and teach you in the way which you should go; I will counsel you with My eye upon you. (Ps. 32:8)

I was enjoying one of southern California's most beautiful beaches. The day was warm, the water was perfect, and the beach was swarming with people. As far as I could see in any direction, there were throngs of people—families, children, couples, teenagers, senior citizens. It was the end of summer, and it seemed like all the world had come to San Diego.

I love to watch the smallest ones dig in the sand and play tag with the waves. Sometimes they win, and sometimes the ocean wins. Today hundreds of little ones played on the shoreline. One strong wave could knock them down, and who would be there to snatch them out of danger? Was anyone paying attention? Then it happened. The surprise wave came, and a small child went under. As I jumped to my feet, his mother had already reached the small child and had scooped him to safety in her loving arms. With all those children in view, how did she see one small child in a vast ocean shoreline? The answer is simple. She saw him because she was his mother, and her eyes were on him continually. She knew her own. I doubt that the child was aware of the protective eyes of his mother, just as we lose awareness of our Father's eyes.

Behold, the eye of the Lord is on those who fear Him, on those who hope for His lovingkindness (Ps. 33:18). Remember that you're His precious child today and always, and He won't let the waves overtake you. Believe it, live it, and then rest in it.

When God Seems Gone

There are some times
when God seems gone,
times I can't explain.

There are some times
I cannot pray
or call upon His name.

There are some times
I'm all alone.
At least, it seems that way.

But God's Word says,
and I believe,
He's with me all my days.

So when those times
are all around
and seek to make me doubt,

I'll look to God,
believe His Word,
and victory will sprout.

—*Carol Hopson*

Questions for Reflection and Obedience

1. Do you really believe you're very precious to God? Why do you think you are or are not?

2. What does Satan use to deceive you into thinking that you're not special?

3. Read Psalm 34, and write out ways God shows His special, protective love to you.

~Day 30~
ARE YOU FRETTING?

Rest in the Lord and wait patiently for Him; do not fret, because of him who prospers in his way, because of the man who carries out wicked schemes. Cease from anger, and forsake wrath; do not fret, it leads only to evildoing.
(Ps. 37:7–8)

As I was watching the evening news, I found that I was becoming more and more angry with what I was hearing from politicians who seem to change their morals and beliefs as quickly as the polls change. I was definitely upset and angry and couldn't get a grip on why this was upsetting me so much. With a major election nearing, I wanted things to go my way. I didn't want to endure the lies and hypocrisy I was exposed to.

Then the Holy Spirit struck me with the cutting edge of God's Word: *"Do not fret, because of him who prospers in his way, because of the man who carries out wicked schemes. Cease from anger."* I suddenly realized that I was sinning with my reaction and frustration. I was going directly against what God's Word tells me to do.

Now you may be facing a different kind of anger or frustration with someone who has wounded you or someone you love so deeply that you feel you will never recover. But God wants to help you through it and give you His strength when you desire it and obey His words (Phil. 4:13).

The reason we need to cease from anger is clear: *"It leads only to evildoing."* Our heavenly Father knows what happens when we harbor bitterness and anger, so He gives us the antidote to anger: Rest in the Lord, and wait for His judgment on those who have betrayed us.

Remember that Jesus is our example: *While being reviled, He did not revile in return; while suffering, He uttered no threats, but kept entrusting Himself to Him who judges righteously* (1 Pet. 2:23).

No More!

My neck is tight, my shoulders ache;
I'm sick as I can be.
The things I've heard, the things I see
are really hurting me.

Each word I hear, each thought I nurse
adds to my misery.
This is not how God's child should feel.
Why can't my mind be free?

Then as I read God's Holy Book,
it pierced me to my soul.
I came to see the choice was mine
to give up my control.

Then let God's peace flow through my life
as I confessed my sin.
And as I gave up all my pain,
He cleansed me from within.

So when my neck gets tight again
and anger's at my door,
I'll trust my Lord, obey His Word,
and walk that road no more!

—*Carol Hopson*

Questions for Reflection and Obedience

1. Are you struggling with anger today? What or who is this anger focused on?

2. Can you see that this anger is sin against God because His Word tells us to cease from anger?

3. Read what the following verses tell us about anger:

   Ephesians 4:31–32

   Colossians 3:8, 12

   Ephesians 4:26

4. If you're ready to have God's peace, confess your sin of anger. Leave the one who has hurt you in God's righteous hands.

CHAPTER 3

CHOOSING A NEW WAY OF LIFE!

To know God's peace, I must love Him above all else and believe His words.

You have just been through thirty days of learning how to make choices that lead to peace. So why, at times, do you still lack peace? Let me share with you why I have lost my peace. It was because I didn't really believe God could give it to me. I didn't believe He could handle my problems in a way I approved of. When I have not had peace, it was because:

- I didn't believe I could be happy living far away

from my children and grandchildren (1 John 1:4).

- I didn't believe I could be happy in a cold, rainy climate (Gal. 5:22).

- I didn't believe God would heal me physically from a prolonged illness (1 Peter 5:10).

- I didn't believe God could give me enough grace to suffer patiently under severe testing (2 Cor. 12:9–10).

- I didn't believe God would provide for our financial needs (Matt. 6:25–34).

- I didn't believe that the things which were happening would work out for my good (Rom. 8:28; John 11:40).

- I didn't believe God's plan was the best plan for my life (Rom. 6:11–13; Phil. 1:6).

In each of these situations in my life, there were moments when I was upset or worried. **The promised peace was gone because I didn't believe God.** When trusted friends or beloved mates betray our trust, we find it difficult to trust them again, and rightly so. But our heavenly Father has never betrayed our trust, and we have no reason to distrust what He says. Our only real reason for not believing is our lack of knowing Him deeply, and we therefore dislike His plan for us. Because we don't like it, because it may be painful, because it doesn't seem fair, because we don't understand it, we decide to throw out all God's promises and therefore God's peace. We have made the choice, not God. God has never promised that the Christian life is problem-free or pain-free, but He promises that He will be with us and give us *peace in the midst* of all we encounter.

Peace I leave with you; My peace I give to you; not as the world gives, do I give to you. Let not your heart be troubled, nor let it be fearful. (John 14:27)

Be anxious for nothing, but in everything by prayer and supplication with thanksgiving let your requests be made known to God. And the peace of God, which surpasses all comprehension, shall guard your hearts and your minds in Christ Jesus. (Phil. 4:6–7)

The steadfast of mind Thou wilt keep in perfect peace, because he trusts in Thee. (Isa. 26:3)

Who You Choose to Trust Makes All the Difference

A young child was caught on the fifth floor of a burning building. She had no escape, and it looked like her life would come to a tragic end. The people below all hollered for her to jump into the firemen's net which was held strategically below. Various firefighters got on the megaphone and tried to convince her to jump. They tried all the tricks and tactics they could think of, but the little girl wouldn't move. She heard them all but wouldn't respond.

Finally, one more man took the megaphone and yelled for her to jump. He told her not to be afraid, the men would catch her, and she would be safe. And without another pause, the little girl jumped safely into the waiting net. Why did she suddenly leave her fear behind? Why did she finally listen and act upon what she heard? Had her situation changed? Had the fire no longer been a threat to her? No. The reason she jumped was because her father was the one who told her she would be okay, and she trusted her father. She knew how much he loved her and that he would not ask her to jump if it wasn't the best thing for her to do. He had proven his love for her time and time again.

Jesus proved His love for you when He hung on that old, rugged cross for your sins and mine. *Greater love has no one than this, that one lay down his life for his friends* (John 15:13). He could have changed the plan and avoided the cross, but He loved you so much that He provided a way of forgiveness for all you've ever done or will do. And because His love was so great, He gave you the Holy Spirit to help convict, teach, guide, and comfort you throughout this life on earth. *And I will ask the Father, and He will give you another Helper, that He may be with you forever; that is the Spirit of truth, whom the world cannot receive, because it does not behold Him or know Him, but you know Him because He abides with you and will be in you* (John 14:16–17). And He went so far beyond that in His love that He secured your future in heaven for all eternity so you could have joy and hope both now and forever.

> *Let not your heart be troubled; believe in God, believe also in Me. In My Father's house are many dwelling places; if it were not so, I would have told you; for I go to prepare a place for you. And if I go and prepare a place for you, I will come again, and receive you to Myself; that where I am, there you may be also* (John 14:1–3).

When we are without peace, we are saying, *"You didn't do enough to prove Your love for me, Jesus. I think I can handle my fears better than You can, and so I choose not to believe You or put my trust in You."* Is that really what you want to say to the One who died and rose again for you?

What Did Gina and Ellen Choose?

Let's look at Gina again. I mentioned her in the introduction. She was miserable, lonely, and bitter because she had to move to a new state, leaving behind their family, friends, church, and home. Why didn't Gina have peace? Because she really didn't know God. She knew about Him, she knew of Him, but she didn't know Him and how much He loved her. Therefore, she didn't believe He could bring her contentment and purpose in this new place. She chose to nurse the pain and curse her husband and God for bringing this about.

In Max Lucado's book *On the Anvil,* he writes:

> For all the things we don't know about Judas, there is one thing we know for sure: He had no relationship with the Master. He had seen Jesus, but he did not know him. He had heard Jesus, but he did not understand him. He had a religion but no relationship.
>
> As Satan worked his way around the table in the upper room, he needed a special kind of man to betray our Lord. He needed a man who had seen Jesus but who did not know him. He needed a man who knew the actions of Jesus but had missed out on the mission of Jesus. Judas was this man. He knew the empire but had never known the Man. . . . Judas bore the cloak of religion, but he never knew the heart of Christ. Let's make it our goal to know . . . deeply (Tyndale, 1985, p. 28).

Gina was one of the many who sit in church each Sunday and even teach Sunday school classes. But they've never had a personal relationship with their Creator. They have a head knowledge that never reaches their hearts; therefore, they have no transforming power in their lives. As Gina understood this, she gave her life completely to the Lord for the first time. And in her brokenness she realized how selfish and foolish she had become. She asked forgiveness from the Lord for her anger and bitterness and then asked the same of her husband and family.

As Gina opened her heart to God's love, she began to fall in love with her Savior. She became aware of her stubbornness and blindness in regard to what God might want to do in and through her in this new place. As she read Philippians 2:5–8, she realized she needed to give up her "rights" and "empty self" so God could fill and use her. When doubts or loneliness came, she went to God's Word for comfort and believed His promises because He was worthy to be trusted.

> *Do not fear, for I am with you; do not anxiously look about you, for I am your God. I will strengthen you, surely I will help you, surely I will uphold you with My righteous right hand. . . . For I am the Lord your God, who upholds your right hand, who says to you, "Do not fear, I will help you." (Isa. 41:10, 13)*

> *"For I know the plans that I have for you," declares the Lord, "plans for welfare and not for calamity to give you a future and a hope." (Jer. 29:11)*

Gina became aware of her daily choices: She could go back to being miserable and trust only in herself, or she could trust Jesus with her life and her future. These are the two choices we are each faced with when we lose our peace. Through many tears, Gina chose to know God and love Him with all her heart and believe His Word.

I met with her several more times and saw an incredible change in her. After only a few weeks, she shared how

CHOOSING A NEW WAY OF LIFE!

much more peaceful her home had become. And, because of sharing her decision with her husband, they had grown closer than ever, and he desired to be the spiritual leader in their home. She told me that her children were reflecting her peace and were growing in their new Christian school. She was excited about the changes she saw in her own attitudes and desires. Her words to me were, "And to think I almost missed all God wanted to do for me and my family because of my stubbornness!"

It's now a year later, and Gina reaches out to other new families in the area. She helps them adjust and make right choices. Gina discovered God's peace and was never the same.

Remember Ellen? She had the unmarried daughter who was pregnant. She thought there would be no more peace or joy for her. She too had a choice to make. She had to be willing to give up her picture of the future, what she thought her family's lives should look like, and accept things as they were. Through counseling and God's precious, living Word, she gave up her pride, her "right" to a perfect family, and accepted her circumstances. *Trust in the Lord with all your heart, and do not lean on your own understanding* (Prov. 3:5).

As Ellen chose to believe that God could make "all things to work together for good" (Rom. 8:28), *she began to desire to be a witness to others by acting upon God's promises rather than reacting to her circumstances.* Of course, there was still pain, but she learned that she could have *peace in the midst* of pain if she believed and lived by Romans 8:28. She began a new love relationship with her Lord; and as a result of that new relationship, God was magnified to others. Those involved were open to hear and receive God's love because of what they observed in Ellen. *He put a new song in my mouth, a song of praise to our God; many will see and fear, and will trust in the Lord* (Ps. 40:3). Her daughter repented, and they formed a bond that was deeper than they'd ever had. And, by placing the baby in a Christian home, they could tearfully rejoice that God had answered the prayers of a childless couple. Ellen is now in a ministry to help other parents who are suddenly faced with crisis.

Peace Is Trusting *in the Midst* of a Storm

When I felt like the world was caving in on me because of painful circumstances, I reread the story of Lazarus many times. You see, Mary and Martha loved Jesus like I did. They were good friends of His, and they believed He would always be there for them. They sent a message to Jesus saying, *Lord, your friend is very ill.* Jesus then told the disciples, *This illness will not end in death; it will bring glory to God— for it will show the glory of the Son of God* (John 11:3–4 Phillips).

The problem was that Mary and Martha didn't hear this. They only saw their beloved brother very ill and wondered why Jesus didn't come. Then Jesus heard that Lazarus died, but He wanted the disciples to understand why He waited to go to him. *Lazarus has died, and I am glad that I was not there—for your sakes, that you may learn to believe. And now, let us go to him* (John 11:15 Phillips). *The Message* reads, *You're about to be given new grounds for believing.*

You may be in Mary and Martha's situation right now. You may be facing a painful situation with a loved one, and you can't see God working. You're in good company. Mary and Martha couldn't see it either. But the truth of God's Word is, He was working! He had a bigger purpose that they did not yet see or understand. So when Jesus came to Bethany, Lazarus had been in the grave four days. Friends had come to offer the women sympathy over their brother's death. Martha ran out first to meet Jesus. When Mary heard that Jesus was asking for her, she jumped up to meet Him. The friends followed to see what Jesus would do, and He was deeply moved by their sadness (v. 33). Jesus asked where they had put Lazarus and went on to the grave while the others followed.

I'm sure many were wondering why Jesus had let this happen to someone He dearly loved when he had healed strangers many times. And I'm sure you wonder why God doesn't heal your situation if He really loves you, especially when you see other people's problems resolved. I remember feeling that way when I had asked Jesus to heal me from a serious illness, and yet it continued month after month. Later, I realized that He was working in me during those long months to have a new understanding and empathy for those who suffer. He was teaching me what living by faith really meant. **I was learning that joy was not based on being healthy but on being in fellowship with my Lord.**

When Jesus asked that men remove the stone from the grave, Martha told Him that by now the body would be decaying. **To her it was too late; but to Jesus it was just the right time.** Now, here's the exciting part. Here's the part that has uplifted my weary heart, the words that have strengthened and encouraged me, the words I have chosen to believe *in the midst: 'Did I not tell you,' replied Jesus, 'that if you believed, you would see the wonder of what God can do?'* (John 11:40 Phillips).

There it is! *If I choose to believe God, I will wait confidently and see the wonder of what He can do.* Jesus raised Lazarus from the dead. He did the impossible, and He can do the same for you. Peace will come when you really believe what He promises. To have peace in the midst is not to be without sorrow in the midst. To have peace is to be without anxiety, anger, frustration, or resentment. To have peace is to know the God you've given your heart to and trust Him to give you purpose and fulfillment *in the midst of your circumstances.* It is choosing to see things from God's perspective when He reveals it to you and trusting His righteous judgment when He doesn't (1 Pet. 2:21–23).

This means tremendous joy to you, even though at present you may be temporarily harassed by all kinds of trials. This is no accident—it happens to prove your faith, which is infinitely more valuable than gold, and gold, as you know, even though it is ultimately perishable, must be purified by fire. This proving of your faith is planned to result in praise and glory and honour in the day when Jesus Christ reveals himself. And though you have never seen him, yet you love him. At present you trust him without being able to see him, and even now he brings you a joy that words cannot express and which has in it a hint of the glories of Heaven. (1 Pet. 1:6–8 Phillips)

Peace then, is your life's personal portrait of faith to hang on the walls of eternity. *But the righteous will live by his faith* (Hab. 2:4). If yesterday's picture of your life isn't what you desired, if it doesn't bring glory to God, if it seems to have no beauty or meaning, why not begin a fresh painting today? It's your choice!

A Portrait of Peace

The picture wasn't restful
as storm clouds gathered 'round.
The winds were blowing sideways,
while rain pelted the ground.

The trees were bending over,
and darkness hovered near.
A waterfall was raging,
swelling banks were cause for fear.

The lonely scene was eerie,
threat'ning clouds would soon release.
And yet this awesome portrait
had been entitled "Peace."

What could the artist mean by this?
It made no sense to me.
And then I caught a glimpse of
something different in the tree.

For tucked inside a giant limb,
a tiny bird found rest
as he was safely hidden in
the comfort of his nest.

Not fearful of the raging storm
nor stressed by all the rain,
this place of true contentment
was where he would remain.

Then I began to see how peace
was like that little nest.
I need not fear the storms of life
but claim God knows what's best.

I'll trust His love when times are tough,
and I don't understand.
I'll give Him praise, then wait and see
the *wonder of His plan.*

*"Did I not tell you," replied Jesus, "that if you believed, you
would see the wonder of what God can do?"*
(John 11:40 *Phillips*)

—*Carol Hopson*

EPILOGUE

The wonder of what God can do!

When I didn't believe I could be happy living far away from my children and grandchildren, God took the pain away and gave me a new outlook on living in a new place. He opened my heart to reach out to others to fill that void, and in return He blessed me with joy beyond human understanding in serving Him. As I've shared the story of leaving my home, grandchildren, friends, ministries, God has repeatedly used that to open women's hearts to hear how God could meet their needs, too.

When I didn't believe I could really be happy in a cold, rainy climate, God taught me through His Word that happiness was not a product of being in the sun but a product of being with the Son. As I chose to accept the rain, gray skies, and new style of living, He opened my eyes to all there was to see and enjoy in a new climate, and I grew to truly love it. God has used this experience many times in my speaking to help others who struggle with where God has placed them.

When I didn't believe God would heal me physically from a prolonged illness, God revealed to me that I needed to accept that this illness was not a mistake in God's eyes. I needed to accept it as part of His good plan for me. This was the way He chose to use me at this time, and I found new ways of serving Him from my bed that gave purpose to my pain. My seminars on "Killing the Giant of Discouragement" came from that illness.

When I didn't believe God could give me enough grace to suffer patiently under severe testing, God showed me that His grace was truly sufficient as I chose to trust Him with my life and future. Then God had me write a "Facing Fear with Faith" journal which has been published in my first book *But God, This Wasn't My Plan*. God has used this faith journal to help and encourage thousands of others who feel they can't go on.

When I didn't believe God would provide for our financial needs, He would always bring in just enough for each day. I learned what it really means to live by faith, and I wouldn't trade that experience for anything. When His timing was right, He moved my husband and me into an incredible Christian ministry where we are joyfully, faithfully serving and seeing His richest blessings.

When I didn't believe that the things which were happening would work out for my good, God taught me to walk by faith, not by sight. He allowed me to speak time and time again on His peace and faithfulness in the midst of our difficult circumstances. Because of the painful situations my husband and I went through, hearts were open to listen to how God had supplied our needs physically, spiritually, and emotionally.

When I didn't believe God's plan was the best plan for my life, God taught me to wait for the wonder of what He would do in any situation I was in and be fruitful and faithful each day. God's best plan has included moving me back to the sunshine, moving me back near my children and gra███ildren (things I never asked Him for). He has blessed m█ ███ ██merous new opportunities to speak for Him. Hi█ ██ █ also included writing three books, all of which ha█ ███████ut of the most difficult but most fruitful days o█

█ ███████ **er of what God will do when we give our**
█

INDEX OF POEMS

Help Me, Lord xii

The Word of God 20

Choices 24

Lord of the Dance 28

Seasons 32

A Servant's Heart 36

The Shield of Faith 39

One Day Closer to Glory 42

But the Good Thing Is! 45

 In the Center of the Circle 48

Wait Again? 51

My New Song 54

Weeds 57

The MRI 60

A Grateful Heart 64

This Isn't Easy, Lord! 68

What Kind of Trophy? 71

Peace 74

God Is in Control! 77

The Yoke of Rest 80

Where Contentment Lies 84

What Matters to God? 88

His Voice 91

It's Your Choice! 94

The Other Side 97

Can You Use Me? 100

Bolt the Door! 104

Will My Father Rejoice? 107

Does It Really Matter? 110

In All My Times 113

When God Seems Gone 117

No More! 121

A Portrait of Peace 133

Carol Hopson welcomes your inquiries regarding speaking engagements.

She can be contacted at:

1015 Olive Crest Dr
Encinitas, CA 92024

E-mail address: logonjah@aol.com

To order additional copies of

in the
Midst

Have your credit card ready and call

toll free **(877) 421-READ (7323)**

or send $9.95 each plus
Shipping & Handling*

Your choice: $4.95 - USPS 1st Class
$3.95 - USPS Book Rate

to

**WinePress Publishing
PO Box 428
Enumclaw, WA 98022**

www.winepresspub.com

* Add $1.00 S&H for each additional book ordered.